The Small Business Library Series

The Complete Book of Small Business Management Forms

The Complete Book of Small Business Management Forms

by Daniel Sitarz

Attorney-at-Law

Nova Publishing Company
Small Business and Consumer Legal Books and Software
Carbondale, Illinois

Editorial assistance by Janet Harris Sitarz, Linda Jorgensen-Buhman, Melanie Bray, and Carol Kelly.
Cover and interior design by Linda Jorgensen-Buhman.
Manufactured in the United States.

ISBN 0-935755-56-X   Book w/CD ($24.95)

Cataloging-in-Publication Data
        Sitarz, Dan, 1948-
            The complete book of small business management forms / by Daniel Sitarz. -- 1st ed.
            p. cm. -- (The small business library). Includes index.
            ISBN 0-935755-56-X, Book/CD Set ($24.95).
            1. Small business--Management--Forms. I. Title. II. Series.
        HF5371.S58 2001   651'.29   QBI01-201307

Nova Publishing Company is dedicated to providing up-to-date and accurate legal information to the
public. All Nova publications are periodically revised to contain the latest available legal information.

1st Edition; 1st Printing   December, 2001

This publication is designed to provide accurate and authoritative information in regard to the subject
matter covered. It is sold with the understanding that the publisher and author are not engaged in
rendering legal, accounting, or other professional services. If legal advice or other expert assistance is
required, the services of a competent professional person should be sought.

*—From a Declaration of Principles jointly adopted by a Committee of
the American Bar Association and a Committee of Publishers*

DISCLAIMER

Because of possible unanticipated changes in governing statutes and case law relating to the application of
any information contained in this book, the author, publisher, and any and all persons or entities involved
in any way in the preparation, publication, sale, or distribution of this book disclaim all responsibility
for the legal effects or consequences of any document prepared or action taken in reliance upon
information contained in this book. No representations, either express or implied, are made or given
regarding the legal consequences of the use of any information contained in this book. Purchasers and
persons intending to use this book for the preparation of any legal documents are advised to check
specifically on the current applicable laws in any jurisdiction in which they intend the documents to
be effective.

Nova Publishing Company
Small Business and Consumer Legal Books and Software
1103 West College Street
Carbondale, IL 62901
Editorial: (800) 748-1175

Distributed by:
National Book Network
4720 Boston Way
Lanham, MD 20706
Orders: (800) 462-6420

Table of Contents

List of Forms-on-CD

CHAPTER 1: Employment Documents and Personnel Forms
Form 1: Application for Employment (Adobe PDF form)
Form 2: Job Description Form (Adobe PDF form)
Form 3: Personnel Form (Adobe PDF form)
Form 4: Employment Contract (text form)
Form 5: Consent to Release Employment Information (text form)
Form 6: Employee Confidentiality Agreement (text form)
Form 7: Employee Patents and Invention Agreement (text form)
Form 8: Employee Performance Review (Adobe PDF form)
Form 9: Employee Absence Report Form (Adobe PDF form)
Form 10: Employee Warning Notice (Adobe PDF form)
Form 11: Family and Medical Leave Form (Adobe PDF form)
Form 12: Independent Contractor Agreement (text form)
Form 13: Contractor Subcontractor Agreement (text form)
   Additional Federal Tax and Workplace Forms
Form 14: Application for Employer Identification Number: IRS Form SS-4
  (Adobe PDF form)
Form 15: Wage and Tax Statement: IRS Form W-2 (Adobe PDF form)
Form 16: Employee's Withholding Allowance Certificate: IRS Form W-4 (Adobe
  PDF form)
Form 17: Employee Eligibility Verification: INS Form I-9 (Adobe PDF form)
Form 18: OSHA Workplace Notice 3165 (Adobe PDF form)

CHAPTER 2: Accounting Forms

Form 19: Financial Recordkeeping Checklist (text form)

Chart of Accounts

Form 20: Income Chart of Accounts (text form)

Form 21: Expense Chart of Accounts (text form)

Form 22: Balance Sheet Chart of Accounts (text form)

Business Bank Accounts and Petty Cash

Form 23: Check Register (Adobe PDF form)

Form 24: Monthly Bank Statement Reconciliation (Adobe PDF form)

Form 25: Petty Cash Register (Adobe PDF form)

Business Assets and Inventory

Form 26: Current Asset Account (Adobe PDF form)

Form 27: Periodic Inventory Record (Adobe PDF form)

Form 28: Perpetual Inventory Record (Adobe PDF form)

Form 29: Physical Inventory Record (Adobe PDF form)

Form 30: Cost of Goods Sold Record (Adobe PDF form)

Form 31: Fixed Asset Account (Adobe PDF form)

Business Debts

Form 32: Accounts Payable Record (Adobe PDF form)

Form 33: Individual Accounts Payable Record (Adobe PDF form)

Form 34: Long-Term Debt Record (Adobe PDF form)

Business Expenses

Form 35: Daily Expense Record (Adobe PDF form)

Form 36: Weekly Expense Record (Adobe PDF form)

Form 37: Monthly Expense Record (Adobe PDF form)

Form 38: Annual Expense Summary (Adobe PDF form)

Form 39: Weekly Travel Expense Record (Adobe PDF form)

Form 40: Monthly Travel Expense Record (Adobe PDF form)

Form 41: Annual Travel Expense Summary (Adobe PDF form)

Form 42: Weekly Auto Expense Record (Adobe PDF form)

Form 43: Monthly Auto Expense Record (Adobe PDF form)

Form 44: Annual Auto Expense Summary (Adobe PDF form)

Form 45: Weekly Meals and Entertainment Expense Record (Adobe PDF form)

Form 46: Monthly Meals and Entertainment Expense Record (Adobe PDF form)

Form 47: Annual Meals and Entertainment Expense Summary (Adobe PDF form)

Form 48: Purchase Order (Adobe PDF form)

Form 49: Purchase Order Record (Adobe PDF form)

Business Income

Form 50: Daily Cash Report (Adobe PDF form)

Form 51: Weekly Cash Report (Adobe PDF form)

Introduction

The purpose of this book is to allow small business owners to have the tools they will need to set up a clear and understandable system with which to manage their businesses. The forms and instructions that are included cover a wide range of business management activities, from hiring and managing employees to setting up an accounting system and from handling income taxes and payroll to setting up marketing plans. In each chapter of this book, you will find an introductory section that will give you an overview of the types of situations in which the forms in that chapter will generally be used. This explanation will, generally, include a listing of the information that must be compiled to complete the form. The forms are not designed to be torn out of this book (especially if this is a library's copy!). By using the copies of the forms that are contained on the attached CD-ROM, it is possible to easily fill in the forms and prepare them for filing or use. If you do not have access to a computer, the preferable manner for using these forms is to make a photocopy of the form, fill in the information that is necessary, and then retype the form in its entirety on white letter-sized paper. If in doubt as to whether a particular form will work in a specific application, please consult a competent lawyer. It may also be wise to consult with an experienced accountant if you have questions regarding the accounting, payroll, or tax forms included in this book.

How to Use the Forms-on-CD

The forms on the Forms-on-CD are provided in two separate formats so that they may be accessed by the widest variety of computer users. First, all of the legal and business forms on the Forms-on-CD are provided as text files in text-only format. These files all have the file extension> .txt. These files contain all of the text of the files in a format that may be used in virtually every available word-processing program, such as Microsoft Word and WordPerfect. When opened in a word-processing program, information may be entered directly into the forms and they may then be printed on your computer's printer. Enter information in the text forms where an asterisk (*) is noted. Delete the asterisk upon entry of your information. In addition, the accounting, IRS tax forms, and certain other forms from this book are provided in Adobe PDF format. This particular format provides the most widely-used cross-platform format for accessing computer files. Files in this format may be opened as images and printed on your computer. However, you cannot fill in the forms within your word-processing program. To open the forms in the PDF format, you will need Adobe Acrobat Reader. This computer program is also included on the Forms-on-CD. In order to install this program on your computer, please follow the instructions below. The files in Adobe PDF format all have the file extension> .pdf.

There are a few system requirements in order to use the Forms-on-CD:
- A PC with a 486 or faster processor
- Microsoft Windows 3.1 or later
- At least 8 MB RAM
- At least 10 MB of hard drive space available to install the forms

To download and use the included Adobe Acrobat Reader 5.0 software, that allows you to view and print the enclosed IRS tax forms and formatted accounting forms, there are additional system requirements:
- A PC with an i486 or Pentium processor
- Windows 95, Windows 98, or Windows NT 4.0 with Service Pak 3.0 or later
- 8 MB RAM on Windows 95 or Windows 98 (16 recommended)
- 16 MB RAM on Windows NT (24 recommended)
- 10 MB of additional available hard drive space to install the software

To install Adobe Acrobat Reader:

1. Insert the Forms-on-CD in your computer's CD-ROM drive. From the Windows Desktop, open Windows Explorer. In the left-hand "All Folders" window of Windows Explorer, locate the drive that contains the Forms-on-CD. The title of the CD is "Mgt Forms."

2. Select the subfolder "Acrobat Reader" by left-clicking your mouse on "+" sign preceding the title "Mgt Forms" and then left-clicking on the name "Acrobat Reader." Hold down the left mouse button while the name "Acrobat Reader" is selected and drag the name icon to the "C-drive" name in the same window (All Folders) of Windows Explorer. Release the mouse button when the "C-drive" name is highlighted. Your computer will copy the Adobe Acrobat Reader installation program to a new folder on your computer's hard drive.

3. Now left-click on the new folder titled "Acrobat Reader" in your computer's C-drive. In the right-hand window, you will see the application file titled "ar500enu.exe." This is the Adobe Acrobat Reader 5.0 Installation file. Double click your left mouse button on this file. Your computer will now install the Adobe Acrobat Reader program and create a Desktop Icon for the Adobe Acrobat Reader program as well as the files and folders required for this program to operate. To access the Forms-on-CD that are in Adobe PDF format, please see the instructions that follow on page 18.

To install all of the Forms to your hard drive:

1. Insert the Forms-on-CD into your computer's CD-ROM drive. From the Windows Desktop, open Windows Explorer. In the left-hand "All Folders" window of Windows Explorer, locate the drive that contains the Forms-on-CD. The title of the CD is "Mgt Forms." Select the subfolder "Forms-on-CD" by left-clicking your mouse on "+" sign preceding the title "Mgt Forms" and then left-clicking on the name "Forms-on-CD."

2. Hold down the left mouse button while the name "Forms-on-CD" is selected and drag the name icon to the "C-drive" name in same window (All Folders) of Windows Explorer. Release the mouse button when the "C-drive" name is highlighted. Your computer will copy all of the folders and forms from the Forms-on-CD to a new folder in your C-drive. In the left-hand "All Folders" window of Windows Explorer, locate the drive that contains the Forms-on-CD.

To open the text forms (located in the Text Forms subfolder) through the Windows WordPad program:

1. Open Windows Explorer from your Desktop. In the left-hand "All Folders" window of Windows Explorer, locate the "Forms-on-CD" folder. Select the subfolder "Text Forms" by left-clicking your mouse on "+" sign preceding the title "Forms-on-CD." The list of forms (by number) should appear in the main right-hand window.

2. Double click with your left mouse button on the form that you would like to work with. The selected form will open in the WordPad program. You may wish to save a copy of the form and rename it, so that you will always have the original form available for later use.

To open the text forms (located in the Text subfolder) in your own word-processing program:

1. Your word processing program must be open. Left click with your mouse on File>Open in the menu bar of your word processing program. In the OPEN FILE>Look In Window, if you have installed the Forms-on-CD to your hard drive, select C:Drive. If you wish to access the Forms-on-CD from the CD itself, select the drive letter of your computer's CD-ROM drive.

2. In the main window, left click with your mouse on the title in the Forms-on-CD folder. Then left click your mouse on "Text Forms." The list of forms (by number) should appear in the main window. Double click with your left mouse button on the form that you would like to work with. The selected form will open in your word processor. You may wish to save a copy of the form and rename it, so that you will always have the original form available for later use.

To access the Adobe PDF forms (located in the Adobe PDF subfolder) in the Adobe Acrobat Reader 4.0 program:

1. You must have already installed the Adobe Acrobat Reader program to your computer's hard drive. See above for installation instructions. Open Windows Explorer from your Desktop. In the left-hand "All Folders" window of Windows Explorer, locate the "Forms-on-CD" folder. Select this folder by left-clicking with your mouse on "+" sign preceding the name "Forms-on-CD." Then left click your mouse on the title "Adobe PDF Forms." The list of forms (by number) should appear in the main right-hand window.

2. Double click with your left mouse button on the form that you would like to work with. The selected form will open in the Adobe Acrobat Reader program. You must print an Adobe PDF form in order to fill it in. You may wish to save a copy of the form and rename it, so that you will always have the original form available for later use.forms from this book have been provided on the enclosed Forms-on-CD for your use if you have access to a computer. Use of the Forms-on-CD will enable you to fill out and print the forms without the tedious task of retyping them.

Forms-on-CD Software Licensing Agreement

By opening the computer CD pouch in the back of this book, you agree to abide by the following conditions which Nova Publishing Company places on the use of the enclosed software. Your payment of the purchase price of this product allows you only the following rights:

You may use the software on a single computer at a single location. You own only the CD itself, not the actual software or files that it contains. Nova Publishing Company retains all rights and ownership of the software and files themselves. You are allowed to copy all of the forms to your computer's hard disk, make a back-up copy of the original disk, and use the forms for your own personal use. You are not allowed to make multiple copies of the software itself, nor are you allowed to transfer the information on the CD to anyone else in any manner, including via any type of electronic transfer or computer network. The software and forms are copyrighted and licensed only to the original purchaser of the book/CD package to use in the above manner. Nova Publishing Company warrants only that the software contains computer files containing copies of forms. No other warranties, express or implied, apply. By opening the CD pouch, you acknowledge that you have read this agreement and agree to be bound by it.

Chapter 1

Employment Documents and Personnel Forms

The forms in this section cover a variety of situations that arise in the area of employment. From hiring an employee to subcontracting work on a job, written documents which outline the party's responsibilities and duties are important for keeping an employment situation on an even keel. The employment contract contained in this chapter may be used and adapted for virtually any employment situation. Of course, it is perfectly legal to hire an employee without a contract at all. In many businesses, this is common practice. However, as job skills and salaries rise and as employees are allowed access to sensitive and confidential business information, written employment contracts are often prudent business practice.

An *independent contractor* may also be hired to perform a job. As opposed to an *employee*, this type of worker is defined as one who maintains his or her own independent business, uses his or her own tools, and does not work under the direct supervision of the person who has hired him or her. A contract for hiring an independent contractor is provided in this chapter.

Application for Employment: This form may be used for any job applicant. This application provides notice that the employer is an equal opportunity employer and that the application will be considered without discrimination. Although very basic, this application provides that an applicant complete the following information:

- Name and address
- Social Security and driver's license numbers
- Job applying for
- Special training or skills

- Educational level with dates and places of attendance
- Previous employer's address and phone
- Prior positions, pay, and reasons for leaving
- Name, address, and phone of personal references
- Emergency notification information
- Certification of applicant of truth and authorization for references to release information
- Signature of applicant

Job Description Form: This form is intended to be used by an employer to describe the actual details of each particular job that will need to be filled. Its purpose is to provide both the employer and the employee with a clear delineation of the duties and relationships that apply to the particular job. This form provides the following:

- Who is completing the form
- Job title
- Brief statement of job
- List of major duties of job
- List of minor duties of job
- To whom employee reports
- People to be supervised by employee

Personnel Form: The purpose of this form is to provide a central record of the hiring, job advancement, and end of employment of any employee. This form should be completed upon the hiring of any employee and should be periodically updated as required. The following information is gathered on this form:

- Name, address, and phone of employee
- Social Security number of employee
- Date hired and starting salary
- W-4 form completion and number of dependents
- Any changes in salary
- Any changes in job position
- Date and reason for leaving employment
- Eligibility for rehiring
- Signature of employer
- Signature of employee upon separation

Employment Contract: This form may be used for any situation in which an employee is hired for a specific job. The issues addressed by this contract are as follows:

- That the employee will perform a certain job and any incidental further duties
- That the employee will be hired for a certain period and for a certain salary
- That the employee will be given certain job benefits (for example, sick pay, vacations, etc.)
- That the employee agrees to abide by the employer's rules and regulations
- That the employee agrees to sign agreements regarding confidentiality and inventions
- That the employee agrees to submit any employment disputes to mediation and arbitration

The information necessary to complete this form is as follows:

- The names and addresses of the employer and employee
- A complete description of the job
- The date the job is to begin and the length of time that the job will last
- The amount of compensation and benefits for the employee (for example, salary, sick pay, vacation, retirement, and insurance benefits)
- The state whose laws will govern the contract

Consent to Release Employment Information: This form is used to obtain an employee's consent to have a previous employer release past job records regarding the employee. This form may be completed by supplying the employee's name and address, the current employer's name and address, and the former employer's name and address.

Employee Confidentiality Agreement: This form may be used in those situations in which it is prudent to have the employee agree not to divulge any business or trade secrets. An employer's business secrets include any information regarding the employer's customers, supplies, finances, research, development or manufacturing processes, or any technical or business information. This form also provides that the employee agrees not to make any unauthorized copies of information or take any business information from the employer's facilities. To prepare this form, simply fill in the employer's and employee's names and addresses.

Employee Patents and Invention Agreement: This form is for use in those situations in which a dispute may arise over who owns an invention which an employee created while on the job for an employer. By this form, the employee agrees to provide the employer with any information about such an invention. In addition, this document serves as an assignment and transfer to the employer of any rights that the employee may have had in any invention created on the job. To prepare this form, simply fill in the employer's and employee's names and addresses.

21

Employee Performance Review: This form is to be used for the periodic monitoring of each employee's performance on the job. It may be used annually, semi-annually, or at some other periodic interval. It provides a clear and concise method to describe the employee's performance by providing a method to rate the following:

- Knowledge of the job, including equipment and systems
- Achievement on the job, including initiative and follow-up
- Employee relations with others, including coworkers and management
- Quality of employee's work, including ability and consistency
- Employee's attitude, including dependability and attendance

Employee Absence Report Form: This is a simple form to be completed for each instance of an employee's absence, whether for holiday, vacation, sickness, or otherwise. It provides a record of the reason for the absence, pay, and other comments regarding the incident.

Employee Warning Notice: This form provides a method to warn an employee with a written notice regarding some violation of company policies, ranging from lateness and absence to misconduct and safety violations. The careful use of this form can provide an employer with important records in the event of the necessity to dismiss an employee for repeated warnings.

Family and Medical Leave Form: This form is to be used to comply with the Federal Family and Medical Leave Act which requires that eligible employees be entitled to up to 12 weeks of unpaid and job-protected leave for certain family and medical reasons. To be eligible, an employee must meet the following conditions:

- Have worked for the company for a total of 12 months (does not need to be consecutive)
- Have worked for the company at least 1,250 hours in the last 12 months
- Have a serious health condition that makes him or her unable to perform his or her job, OR
- Have a child, spouse, or parent with a serious health condition that requires the employee's full-time care, OR
- Have a child which after birth, adoption, or foster care requires full-time attention of the employee (whether employee is father or mother)

Independent Contractor Agreement: This form should be used when hiring an independent contractor. It provides a standard form for the hiring out of specific work to be performed within a set time period for a particular payment. It also provides a method for authorizing extra work under the contract. Finally, this document provides that the contractor agrees to indemnify the owner against any claims or liabilities arising from the performance of the work. To complete this form, fill in a detailed description of the work, dates by which portions of the job are to be completed, the pay for the job, the terms and dates of payment, and the state whose laws will govern the contract.

Contractor/Subcontractor Agreement: This form is intended to be used by an independent contractor to hire a subcontractor to perform certain work on a job that the contractor has agreed to perform. It provides for the "farming" out of specific work to be performed by the subcontractor within a set time period for a particular payment. It also provides a method for authorizing extra work under the contract. Finally, this document provides that the subcontractor agrees to indemnify the contractor against any claims or liabilities arising from the performance of the work. To complete this form, fill in a detailed description of the work, dates by which portions of the job are to be completed, the pay for the job, the terms and dates of payment, and the state whose laws will govern the contract.

Application for Employment

Name _____

Address _____

Social Security number _____ Driver's License number _____

Position applying for: _____

Date available: _____

Full time _____ Part time _____ Flexible _____

Special job skills or qualifications: _____

_____

Education

	School	Course of study	Last year	Graduated
High School	_____	_____	_____	_____
College/University	_____	_____	_____	_____
Trade/Vocational	_____	_____	_____	_____
Other	_____	_____	_____	_____
	_____	_____	_____	_____

Employment

Present or previous employer _____

Address _____

Phone _____

Employed from _____ to _____ Position _____

Leaving salary _____ Reason for leaving _____

Past employer _____

Address _____

Phone _____

Employed from _____ to _____ Position _____

Leaving salary _____ Reason for leaving _____

Past employer _____

Address _____

Phone _____

Employed from _____ to _____ Position _____

Leaving salary _____ Reason for leaving _____

May we contact your present employer?   Yes _____   No _____

References

Name _____   Name _____
Address _____   Address _____
Phone _____   Phone _____
Occupation _____   Occupation _____
Relationship _____   Relationship _____

Emergency Notification

In the event of an emergency, I authorize the company to contact the following person:

Name _____
Address _____
Phone _____
Relationship _____

If the company is unable to notify such person, the company may notify the following person:

Name _____
Address _____
Phone _____
Relationship _____

I certify that the information in this application is correct and complete to the best of my knowledge and I understand that intentionally falsifying information could result in refusal of employment or discharge from employment. I also authorize the employers, schools, and individuals named above to provide information to my prospective employer regarding my employment, education, character, and qualifications.

_____   _____
Signature of Applicant   Date

This company is an equal opportunity employer. Your application will be considered without regard to race, age, color, gender, religion, national origin, marital status, ancestry, citizenship, veteran status, or physical or mental disability.

Job Description Form

Date: _____

Prepared by: _____
Title: _____
Department: _____
Approved by: _____

Job Description

Job title: _____
Reporting to: _____
Job statement: _____

Major Duties

1. _____
2. _____
3. _____
4. _____
5. _____
6. _____
7. _____
8. _____
9. _____

Minor Duties

1. _____
2. _____
3. _____
4. _____
5. _____
6. _____
7. _____
8. _____
9. _____

Relationships

Department head: _____
Direct supervisor: _____
People supervised: _____

Personnel Form

Employee name _____
Social Security number _____
Address _____
Phone _____

Date hired _____   Starting salary _____
W-4 Form completed _____   Employee Handbook received ___
Number of dependents_____

Changes in salary	New salary	Date begun
_____	_____	_____
_____	_____	_____
_____	_____	_____

Changes in position	New position	Date begun
_____	_____	_____
_____	_____	_____

Job reviews	Date	Status
_____	_____	_____
_____	_____	_____

Separation	Date	Reason
_____	_____	_____
_____	_____	_____

Laid off _____ Left voluntarily _____
Discharged for cause _____ Discharged for lack of work _____
Other_____

Eligible for rehire? Yes ____   No ____

_____   _____
Signature of Employer   Date

_____   _____
Separation Signature of Employee   Date

Employment Contract

This Contract is made on _____ , 20 _____ , between _____ ,
Employer, of _____ , City of _____ , State of
_____ , and _____ , Employee, of _____ ,
City of _____ , State of _____ .

For valuable consideration, the Employer and Employee agree as follows:

1. The Employee agrees to perform the following duties and job description:

   The Employee also agrees to perform further duties incidental to the general job description. This is considered a full-time position.

2. The Employee will begin work on _____ , 20 _____ . This position shall continue for a period of _____ .

3. The Employee will be paid the following:

   Weekly salary: $ _____

   The Employee will also be given the following benefits:

   Sick pay   _____
   Vacations   _____
   Bonuses   _____
   Retirement benefits   _____
   Insurance benefits   _____

4. The Employee agrees to abide by all rules and regulations of the Employer at all times while employed.

5. This Contract may be terminated by:

   (a) Breach of this Contract by the Employee
   (b) The expiration of this Contract without renewal
   (c) Death of the Employee
   (d) Incapacitation of the Employee for over _____ days in any one year

6. The Employee agrees to sign the following additional documents as a condition to obtaining employment:

   (a) Employee Confidentiality Agreement
   (b) Employee Patents and Invention Agreement

7. Any dispute between the Employer and Employee related to this Contract will be settled by voluntary mediation. If mediation is unsuccessful, the dispute will be settled by binding arbitration using an arbitrator of the American Arbitration Association.

8. Any additional terms of this Contract:

9. No modification of this Contract will be effective unless it is in writing and is signed by both the Employer and Employee. This Contract binds and benefits both parties and any successors. Time is of the essence of this Contract. This document is the entire agreement between the parties. This Contract is governed by the laws of the State of _____ .

Dated: _____ , 20 ____

_____
Signature of Employer

_____
Name of Employer

_____
Signature of Employee

_____
Name of Employee

Consent to Release Employment Information

I, _____ , of _____ , City of _____ , State of _____ , do consent and authorize _____ , of _____ , City of _____ , State of _____ , to release any and all employment records of mine that they might have in their possession to _____ , of _____ , City of _____ , State of _____ .

I release the above party from any liability for the release of any information or records based on this consent and authorization.

Dated: _____ , 20 ____

_____
Signature of Employee

_____
Name of Employee

Employee Confidentiality Agreement

This Agreement is made on _____ , 20 ____ , between _____ , Employer, of _____ , City of _____ , State of _____ , and _____ , Employee, of _____ , City of _____ , State of _____ .

For valuable consideration, the Employer and Employee agree as follows:

1. The Employee agrees to keep all of the Employer's business secrets confidential at all times during and after the term of Employee's employment. Employer's business secrets include any information regarding the Employer's customers, supplies, finances, research, development, manufacturing processes, or any other technical or business information.

2. The Employee agrees not to make any unauthorized copies of any of Employer's business secrets or information without Employer's consent, nor to remove any of Employer's business secrets or information from the Employer's facilities.

3. The parties agree to the following additional terms:

Dated: _____ , 20 ____

_____
Signature of Employer

_____
Name of Employer

_____
Signature of Employee

_____
Name of Employee

Employee Patents and Invention Agreement

This Agreement is made on _____ , 20 ____ , between
_____ , Employer, of _____ , City of _____ ,
State of _____ , and _____ , Employee, of
_____ , City of _____ , State of _____ .

For valuable consideration, the Employer and Employee agree as follows:

1. The Employee agrees to promptly furnish the Employer with a complete record of any inventions or patents which the Employee may create or devise during employment with the Employer.

2. The Employee grants and assigns to the Employer his or her entire rights and interest in any inventions or patents that result in any way from any work performed while employed by the Employer. The Employee agrees that he or she does not have any past employment agreements, patents, or inventions that might conflict with this assignment. The Employer also agrees to sign any further documents necessary to allow the Employer the rights, title, or patent to any such inventions or creations.

3. The parties agree to the following additional terms:

Dated: _____ , 20 ____

_____
Signature of Employer

_____
Name of Employer

_____
Signature of Employee

_____
Name of Employee

Employee Performance Review

Employee name _____
Social Security number _____   Job title _____
Department _____   Date hired _____
Current salary _____   Date of last increase _____
Date of this review _____   Date of last review _____

Review Areas

Comments _____

	Poor	Fair	Good	Excellent
Knowledge of job				
Equipment	_____	_____	_____	_____
Systems	_____	_____	_____	_____
Achievement of job				
Initiative	_____	_____	_____	_____
Follow-up	_____	_____	_____	_____
Employee relations				
With management	_____	_____	_____	_____
With coworkers	_____	_____	_____	_____
Quality of work				
Ability	_____	_____	_____	_____
Consistency	_____	_____	_____	_____
Attitude				
Dependability	_____	_____	_____	_____
Attendance	_____	_____	_____	_____

Reviewer's comments _____

_____   _____
Signature of Reviewer   Date

Was this review discussed with employee? Yes _____   No _____

Employee's Comments _____

_____   _____
Signature of Employee   Date

Employee Absence Report Form

Employee name _____
Social Security number _____ Job title _____
Department _____ Date hired _____

Date(s) of Absence

With pay   *Without pay*

_____   _____
_____   _____
_____   _____

Reason for Absence

Holiday   _____
Vacation   _____
Sickness   _____
Other   _____
               _____

Comments _____
_____
_____

_____   _____
Signature of Employee   Date

Approved by _____   Date _____

Employee Warning Notice

Date of warning _____   Time of warning _____

Employee name _____
Social Security number _____   Job title _____
Department _____   Date hired _____

	Nature of Violation	Remarks
Lateness	_____	_____
Conduct	_____	_____
Absence	_____	_____
Attitude	_____	_____
Disobedience	_____	_____
Carelessness	_____	_____
Safety	_____	_____
Defective work	_____	_____
Cleanliness	_____	_____
Other	_____	_____

_____   _____
Signature of Employer   Date

I have read and understand this warning.

_____   _____
Signature of Employee   Date

Family and Medical Leave Form

Date of request _____

Employee name _____

Social Security number _____   Job title _____

Department _____   Date hired _____

Under the Federal Family and Medical Leave Act (FMLA), eligible employees are entitled to up to 12 (twelve) weeks of unpaid, job-protected leave for certain family and medical reasons. Please submit this request form to your supervisor at leave 30 (thirty) days before the leave is to begin, if possible. When submission of this form 30 (thirty) days in advance is not possible, submit the request as early as possible. The employer reserves the right to deny or postpone leave for failure to give appropriate notice whenever such denial or postponement would be permitted under federal or state law.

Eligibility

	Yes	No
1. Have you worked for the company for a total of 12 months or more (whether or not consecutively)?	___	___
2. During the past 12 months, have you worked at least 1,250 hours?	___	___
3. Have you previously received medical or family leave? If yes, explain:	___	___

Dates of previous leave: From _____ to _____
Purpose of leave: _____

_____

4. Have you taken any intermittent leave?   ___   ___
   If yes, explain: _____

_____

5. Have you taken other time off from your scheduled   ___   ___
   work? If yes, explain: _____

_____

Reasons for Requested Leave

____ Serious health condition that makes you unable to perform your job

Explain: _____

_____

____ Serious health condition of child, spouse, or parent

Explain: _____

_____

____ Care for child after birth, adoption, or foster care

Explain: _____

_____

Dates of requested leave: From: _____ To:_____

I agree to return to work on _____ . If any circumstances change and I am unable to return to work on that date, I agree to inform my employer immediately in writing. I understand that my benefits will continue during my leave and that I will arrange to pay my share of any benefit premiums.

_____   _____
Signature of Employee   Date

Approved   _____
Denied   _____

_____   _____
Signature of Employer   Date

Independent Contractor Agreement

This Agreement is made on _____ , 20 ____ , between _____ , Owner, of _____ , City of _____ , State of _____ , and _____ , Contractor, of _____ , City of _____ , State of _____ .

For valuable consideration, the Owner and Contractor agree as follows:

1. The Contractor agrees to furnish all of the labor and materials to do the following work for the Owner as an independent contractor:

2. The Contractor agrees that the following portions of the total work will be completed by the dates specified:

Work	Date

3. The Contractor agrees to perform this work in a workmanlike manner according to standard practices. If any plans or specifications are part of this job, they are attached to and are part of this Contract.

4. The Owner agrees to pay the Contractor as full payment $ _____ for doing the work outlined above. This price will be paid to the Contractor on satisfactory completion of the work in the following manner and on the following dates:

5. The Contractor and Owner may agree to extra services and work, but any such extras must be set out and agreed to in writing by both the Contractor and the Owner.

6. The Contractor agrees to indemnify and hold the Owner harmless from any claims or liability arising from the Contractor's work under this Contract.

7. No modification of this Contract will be effective unless it is in writing and is signed by both parties. This Contract binds and benefits both parties and any successors. Time is of the essence of this Contract. This document, including any attachments, is the entire agreement between the parties. This Contract is governed by the laws of the State of _____ .

Dated: _____ , 20 ____

_____
Signature of Owner

_____
Name of Owner

_____
Signature of Contractor

_____
Name of Contractor

Contractor/Subcontractor Agreement

This Agreement is made on _____ , 20 ____ , between
_____ , Contractor, of _____ , City of _____ ,
State of _____ , and _____ , Subcontractor, of
_____ , City of _____ , State of _____ .

1. The Subcontractor, as an independent contractor, agrees to furnish all
   of the labor and materials to do the following portions of the work
   specified in the Agreement between the Contractor and the Owner
   dated _____ , 20 ____ :

2. The Subcontractor agrees that the following portions of the total work
   will be completed by the dates specified:

Work	*Date*
_____	_____
_____	_____
_____	_____
_____	_____
_____	_____
_____	_____
_____	_____

3. The Subcontractor agrees to perform this work in a workmanlike
   manner according to standard practices. If any plans or specifications
   are part of this job, they are attached to and are part of this Contract.

4. The Contractor agrees to pay the Subcontractor as full payment $ _____ for doing the work outlined above. This price will be paid to the Subcontractor on satisfactory completion of the work in the following manner and on the following dates:

5. The Contractor and Subcontractor may agree to extra services and work, but any such extras must be set out and agreed to in writing by both the Contractor and the Subcontractor.

6. The Subcontractor agrees to indemnify and hold the Contractor harmless from any claims or liability arising from the Subcontractor's work under this Contract.

7. No modification of this Agreement will be effective unless it is in writing and is signed by both parties. This Agreement binds and benefits both parties and any successors. Time is of the essence of this Agreement. This document, including any attachments, is the entire agreement between the parties. This Agreement is governed by the laws of the State of _____ .

Dated: _____ , 20 ____

_____
Signature of Contractor

_____
Name of Contractor

_____
Signature of Subontractor

_____
Name of Subcontractor

Additional Federal Tax and Workplace Forms

Application for Employee Identification Number (IRS Form SS-4): This form is a mandatory federal form which must be used by any employer to register with the IRS for purposes of payroll tax reporting. Regardless of whether the employer is a sole proprietorship, corporation, partnership, limited liability company, trust, estate, church, school, non-profit organization, or government agency, this form must be completed. Instructions are included on the enclosed Forms-on-CD.

Wage and Tax Statement (IRS Form W-2): This is the familiar form that each employer must provide to each employee in January or February of each calendar year which details the employee's earnings and payroll deductions. A copy of this form is also provided to the Social Security Administration by the employer. Please note that the form provided in this book and on the accompanying CD is *NOT* acceptable for use. The actual printed IRS form *MUST* be used as it is printed on special paper with special machine-readable inks. The W-2 form provided is for informational purposes only and should not be reproduced either by your computer's printer or by a copy machine. You may order an IRS W-2 form either by calling 1-800-TAX-FORM or by visiting the IRS website at www.irs.gov.

Employee's Withholding Allowance Certificate (IRS Form W-4): This form is to be completed by each new employee. Its purpose is to allow the employer to withhold the correct amount of payroll taxes for the employee. The instructions include a simple worksheet that allows the employee to complete the form with ease.

Employment Eligibility Verification (INS Form I-9): This form is required by the U.S. Immigration and Naturalization Service to be completed for each new employee. Its purpose is to verify the citizenship or ability to legally work in the U.S. for each new employee hired after 1986. The completed I-9 Form and a copy of the verifying documents are to be kept in the employee's permanent records for at least three years or one year after employment ends, whichever is shorter. This form is not to be filed with the U.S. INS. In addition, the employer may not use any information supplied by the applicant to discriminate against hiring the employee, if they are eligible for employment in the U.S. Finally, the employer must accept any document from the applicant that fulfills the qualification on the included list of acceptable documents. Instructions are included on the enclosed Forms-on-CD.

OSHA Workplace Notice 3165: This notice is required to be posted in every American workplace by the U.S. Occupational Safety and Health Administration. It specifies the various rights that an employee has under the various OSHA regulations relating to workplace safety.

Form SS-4

(Rev. April 2000)
Department of the Treasury
Internal Revenue Service

Application for Employer Identification Number

(For use by employers, corporations, partnerships, trusts, estates, churches, government agencies, certain individuals, and others. See instructions.)

▶ Keep a copy for your records.

EIN

OMB No. 1545-0003

Please type or print clearly.

1 Name of applicant (legal name) (see instructions)

2 Trade name of business (if different from name on line 1)

3 Executor, trustee, "care of" name

4a Mailing address (street address) (room, apt., or suite no.)

5a Business address (if different from address on lines 4a and 4b)

4b City, state, and ZIP code

5b City, state, and ZIP code

6 County and state where principal business is located

7 Name of principal officer, general partner, grantor, owner, or trustor—SSN or ITIN may be required (see instructions) ▶

8a Type of entity (Check only one box.) (see instructions)

Caution: *If applicant is a limited liability company, see the instructions for line 8a.*

☐ Sole proprietor (SSN) _____
☐ Partnership   ☐ Personal service corp.
☐ REMIC   ☐ National Guard
☐ State/local government   ☐ Farmers' cooperative
☐ Church or church-controlled organization
☐ Other nonprofit organization (specify) ▶ _____
☐ Other (specify) ▶

☐ Estate (SSN of decedent) _____
☐ Plan administrator (SSN) _____
☐ Other corporation (specify) ▶ _____
☐ Trust
☐ Federal government/military
          (enter GEN if applicable) _____

8b If a corporation, name the state or foreign country (if applicable) where incorporated

State	Foreign country

9 Reason for applying (Check only one box.) (see instructions)
☐ Started new business (specify type) ▶ _____

☐ Hired employees (Check the box and see line 12.)
☐ Created a pension plan (specify type) ▶

☐ Banking purpose (specify purpose) ▶ _____
☐ Changed type of organization (specify new type) ▶ _____
☐ Purchased going business
☐ Created a trust (specify type) ▶ _____
☐ Other (specify) ▶

10 Date business started or acquired (month, day, year) (see instructions)

11 Closing month of accounting year (see instructions)

12 First date wages or annuities were paid or will be paid (month, day, year). **Note:** *If applicant is a withholding agent, enter date income will first be paid to nonresident alien. (month, day, year)* . . . . ▶

	Nonagricultural	Agricultural	Household
13 Highest number of employees expected in the next 12 months. **Note:** *If the applicant does not expect to have any employees during the period, enter -0-. (see instructions)* . . . . ▶			

14 Principal activity (see instructions) ▶

15 Is the principal business activity manufacturing? . . . .   ☐ Yes ☐ No
If "Yes," principal product and raw material used ▶

16 To whom are most of the products or services sold? Please check one box.   ☐ Business (wholesale)
☐ Public (retail)   ☐ Other (specify) ▶   ☐ N/A

17a Has the applicant ever applied for an employer identification number for this or any other business? . . . .   ☐ Yes ☐ No
Note: *If "Yes," please complete lines 17b and 17c.*

17b If you checked "Yes" on line 17a, give applicant's legal name and trade name shown on prior application, if different from line 1 or 2 above.
Legal name ▶   Trade name ▶

17c Approximate date when and city and state where the application was filed. Enter previous employer identification number if known.

Approximate date when filed (mo., day, year)	City and state where filed	Previous EIN

Under penalties of perjury, I declare that I have examined this application, and to the best of my knowledge and belief, it is true, correct, and complete.

Business telephone number (include area code)
( )

Fax telephone number (include area code)
( )

Name and title (Please type or print clearly.) ▶

Signature ▶   Date ▶

Note: *Do not write below this line. For official use only.*

Please leave blank ▶	Geo.	Ind.	Class	Size	Reason for applying

For Privacy Act and Paperwork Reduction Act Notice, see page 4.   Cat. No. 16055N   Form **SS-4** (Rev. 4-2000)

Attention!

This form is provided for informational purposes and should not be reproduced on personal computer printers or copy machines by individual taxpayers for filing. The printed version of this form is a "machine readable" form. As such, it must be printed using special paper, special inks, and within precise specifications.

---

a Control number	22222	Void ☐	For Official Use Only ▶ OMB No. 1545-0008		
b Employer identification number				**1** Wages, tips, other compensation $	**2** Federal income tax withheld $
c Employer's name, address, and ZIP code				**3** Social security wages $	**4** Social security tax withheld $
				5 Medicare wages and tips $	**6** Medicare tax withheld $
				7 Social security tips $	**8** Allocated tips $
d Employee's social security number				**9** Advance EIC payment $	**10** Dependent care benefits $
e Employee's first name and initial / Last name				**11** Nonqualified plans $	**12a** See instructions for box 12 $
				13 Statutory employee ☐ Retirement plan ☐ Third-party sick pay ☐	**12b** $
				14 Other	**12c** $
					12d $
f Employee's address and ZIP code					

15 State Employer's state ID number	16 State wages, tips, etc. $	17 State income tax $	18 Local wages, tips, etc. $	19 Local income tax $	20 Locality name
	$	$	$	$	

Form **W-2** Wage and Tax Statement **2001** Department of the Treasury—Internal Revenue Service

Copy A For Social Security Administration—Send this entire page with Form W-3 to the Social Security Administration; photocopies are **not** acceptable.

Cat. No. 10134D

For Privacy Act and Paperwork Reduction Act Notice, see separate instructions.

Do Not Cut, Fold, or Staple Forms on This Page — Do Not Cut, Fold, or Staple Forms on This Page

Employers, Please Note-

Specific information needed to complete Form W-2 is given in a separate booklet titled **2001 Instructions for Forms W-2 and W-3.** You can order those instructions and additional forms by calling 1-800-TAX-FORM (1-800-829-3676). You can also get forms and instructions from the IRS Web Site at **www.irs.gov.**

Caution: *Because the SSA processes paper forms by machine, you cannot file with the SSA Forms W-2 and W-3 that you print from the IRS Web Site.*

Due dates. Furnish Copies B, C, and 2 to the employee generally by January 31, 2002.

File Copy A with the SSA generally by February 28, 2002. Send all Copies A with **Form W-3,** Transmittal of Wage and Tax Statements. However, if you file electronically (not by magnetic media), the due date is April 1, 2002.

Form W-4 (2001)

Purpose. Complete Form W-4 so your employer can withhold the correct Federal income tax from your pay. Because your tax situation may change, you may want to refigure your withholding each year.

Exemption from withholding. If you are exempt, complete only lines 1, 2, 3, 4, and 7, and sign the form to validate it. Your exemption for 2001 expires February 18, 2002.

Note: *You cannot claim exemption from withholding if (1) your income exceeds $750 and includes more than $250 of unearned income (e.g., interest and dividends) and (2) another person can claim you as a dependent on their tax return.*

Basic instructions. If you are not exempt, complete the **Personal Allowances Worksheet** below. The worksheets on page 2 adjust your withholding allowances based on itemized deductions, certain credits, adjustments to income, or two-earner/two-job situations. Complete all worksheets that apply. They will help you figure the number of withholding allowances you are entitled to claim. **However, you may claim fewer (or zero) allowances.**

Head of household. Generally, you may claim head of household filing status on your tax return only if you are unmarried and pay more than 50% of the costs of keeping up a home for yourself and your dependent(s) or other qualifying individuals. See line E below.

Tax credits. You can take projected tax credits into account in figuring your allowable number of withholding allowances. Credits for child or dependent care expenses and the child tax credit may be claimed using the **Personal Allowances Worksheet** below. See Pub. 919, **How Do I Adjust My Tax Withholding?** for information on converting your other credits into withholding allowances.

Nonwage income. If you have a large amount of nonwage income, such as interest or dividends, consider making estimated tax payments using **Form 1040-ES,** Estimated Tax for Individuals. Otherwise, you may owe additional tax.

Two earners/two jobs. If you have a working spouse or more than one job, figure the total number of allowances you are entitled to claim on all jobs using worksheets from only one Form W-4. Your withholding usually will be most accurate when all allowances are claimed on the Form W-4 for the highest paying job and zero allowances are claimed on the others.

Check your withholding. After your Form W-4 takes effect, use Pub. 919 to see how the dollar amount you are having withheld compares to your projected total tax for 2001. Get Pub. 919 especially if you used the **Two-Earner/Two-Job Worksheet** on page 2 and your earnings exceed $150,000 (Single) or $200,000 (Married).

Recent name change? If your name on line 1 differs from that shown on your social security card, call 1-800-772-1213 for a new social security card.

Personal Allowances Worksheet (Keep for your records.)

A   Enter "1" for **yourself** if no one else can claim you as a dependent . . . . A _____

B   Enter "1" if: { • You are single and have only one job; or
         • You are married, have only one job, and your spouse does not work; or } . . B _____
         • Your wages from a second job or your spouse's wages (or the total of both) are $1,000 or less.

C   Enter "1" for your **spouse.** But, you may choose to enter -0- if you are married and have either a working spouse or more than one job. (Entering -0- may help you avoid having too little tax withheld.) . . . . C _____

D   Enter number of **dependents** (other than your spouse or yourself) you will claim on your tax return . . . . D _____

E   Enter "1" if you will file as **head of household** on your tax return (see conditions under **Head of household** above) . E _____

F   Enter "1" if you have at least $1,500 of **child or dependent care expenses** for which you plan to claim a credit . . F _____
    (**Note:** *Do not include child support payments. See **Pub. 503,** Child and Dependent Care Expenses, for details.*)

G   **Child Tax Credit** (including additional child tax credit):
    • If your total income will be between $18,000 and $50,000 ($23,000 and $63,000 if married), enter "1" for each eligible child.
    • If your total income will be between $50,000 and $80,000 ($63,000 and $115,000 if married), enter "1" if you have two
      eligible children, enter "2" if you have three or four eligible children, or enter "3" if you have five or more eligible children.   G _____

H   Add lines A through G and enter total here. (**Note:** *This may be different from the number of exemptions you claim on your tax return.*) ▶   H _____

| For accuracy, complete all worksheets that apply. | • If you plan to **itemize or claim adjustments to income** and want to reduce your withholding, see the **Deductions and Adjustments Worksheet** on page 2.
• If you are **single,** have **more than one job** and your combined earnings from all jobs exceed $35,000, **or** if you are **married** and have a **working spouse or more than one job** and the combined earnings from all jobs exceed $60,000, see the **Two-Earner/Two-Job Worksheet** on page 2 to avoid having too little tax withheld.
• If **neither** of the above situations applies, **stop here** and enter the number from line H on line 5 of Form W-4 below. |

- - - - - - - - - - - - - - - - -   **Cut here and give Form W-4 to your employer. Keep the top part for your records.**   - - - - - - - - - - - - - - -

| Form **W-4**
Department of the Treasury
Internal Revenue Service | **Employee's Withholding Allowance Certificate**
▶ **For Privacy Act and Paperwork Reduction Act Notice, see page 2.** | OMB No. 1545-0010
2001 |

| 1   Type or print your first name and middle initial   Last name | 2   Your social security number |

Home address (number and street or rural route)
3   ☐ Single   ☐ Married   ☐ Married, but withhold at higher Single rate.
    Note: *if married, but legally separated, or spouse is a nonresident alien, check the Single box.*

City or town, state, and ZIP code
4   If your last name differs from that on your social security card, check here. You must call 1-800-772-1213 for a new card. ▶ ☐

5   Total number of allowances you are claiming (from line **H** above **or** from the applicable worksheet on page 2)   **5** ____

6   Additional amount, if any, you want withheld from each paycheck . . . . **6** $____

7   I claim exemption from withholding for 2001, and I certify that I meet **both** of the following conditions for exemption:
   • Last year I had a right to a refund of **all** Federal income tax withheld because I had **no** tax liability **and**
   • This year I expect a refund of **all** Federal income tax withheld because I expect to have **no** tax liability.
   If you meet both conditions, write "Exempt" here . . . . ▶ | **7** |

Under penalties of perjury, I certify that I am entitled to the number of withholding allowances claimed on this certificate, or I am entitled to claim exempt status.

Employee's signature
(Form is not valid unless you sign it.) ▶   Date ▶

| 8   Employer's name and address (Employer: Complete lines 8 and 10 only if sending to the IRS.) | 9   Office code (optional) | 10   Employer identification number |

Cat. No. 10220Q

Deductions and Adjustments Worksheet

Note: *Use this worksheet only if you plan to itemize deductions, claim certain credits, or claim adjustments to income on your 2001 tax return.*

1 Enter an estimate of your 2001 itemized deductions. These include qualifying home mortgage interest, charitable contributions, state and local taxes, medical expenses in excess of 7.5% of your income, and miscellaneous deductions. (For 2001, you may have to reduce your itemized deductions if your income is over $132,950 ($66,475 if married filing separately). See **Worksheet 3** in Pub. 919 for details.) . . .   **1** $ _____

2 Enter: { $7,600 if married filing jointly or qualifying widow(er)
            $6,650 if head of household
            $4,550 if single
            $3,800 if married filing separately }   . . . .   **2** $ _____

3 **Subtract** line 2 from line 1. If line 2 is greater than line 1, enter -0- . . . . . .   **3** $ _____

4 Enter an estimate of your 2001 adjustments to income, including alimony, deductible IRA contributions, and student loan interest   **4** $ _____

5 **Add** lines 3 and 4 and enter the total (Include any amount for credits from **Worksheet 7** in Pub. 919.) .   **5** $ _____

6 Enter an estimate of your 2001 nonwage income (such as dividends or interest) . . . .   **6** $ _____

7 **Subtract** line 6 from line 5. Enter the result, but not less than -0- . . . .   **7** $ _____

8 **Divide** the amount on line 7 by $3,000 and enter the result here. Drop any fraction . . . . .   **8** _____

9 Enter the number from the **Personal Allowances Worksheet**, line H, page 1 . . . . . .   **9** _____

10 **Add** lines 8 and 9 and enter the total here. If you plan to use the **Two-Earner/Two-Job Worksheet,** also enter this total on line 1 below. Otherwise, **stop here** and enter this total on Form W-4, line 5, page 1 .   **10** _____

Two-Earner/Two-Job Worksheet

Note: *Use this worksheet only if the instructions under line H on page 1 direct you here.*

1 Enter the number from line H, page 1 (or from line 10 above if you used the **Deductions and Adjustments Worksheet**)   **1** _____

2 Find the number in **Table 1** below that applies to the **lowest** paying job and enter it here . . . . .   **2** _____

3 If line 1 is **more than or equal to** line 2, subtract line 2 from line 1. Enter the result here (if zero, enter -0-) and on Form W-4, line 5, page 1. **Do not** use the rest of this worksheet . . . . . .   **3** _____

Note: *If line 1 is **less than** line 2, enter -0- on Form W-4, line 5, page 1. Complete lines 4–9 below to calculate the additional withholding amount necessary to avoid a year end tax bill.*

4 Enter the number from line 2 of this worksheet . . . .   **4** _____

5 Enter the number from line 1 of this worksheet . . . .   **5** _____

6 **Subtract** line 5 from line 4 . . . .   **6** _____

7 Find the amount in **Table 2** below that applies to the **highest** paying job and enter it here . . . . .   **7** $ _____

8 **Multiply** line 7 by line 6 and enter the result here. This is the additional annual withholding needed . .   **8** $ _____

9 Divide line 8 by the number of pay periods remaining in 2001. For example, divide by 26 if you are paid every two weeks and you complete this form in December 2000. Enter the result here and on Form W-4, line 6, page 1. This is the additional amount to be withheld from each paycheck . . . .   **9** $ _____

Table 1: Two-Earner/Two-Job Worksheet

Married Filing Jointly				All Others			
If wages from **LOWEST** paying job are—	Enter on line 2 above	If wages from **LOWEST** paying job are—	Enter on line 2 above	If wages from **LOWEST** paying job are—	Enter on line 2 above	If wages from **LOWEST** paying job are—	Enter on line 2 above
$0 - $4,000	0	42,001 - 47,000	8	$0 - $6,000	0	65,001 - 80,000	8
4,001 - 8,000	1	47,001 - 55,000	9	6,001 - 12,000	1	80,001 - 105,000	9
8,001 - 14,000	2	55,001 - 65,000	10	12,001 - 17,000	2	105,001 and over	10
14,001 - 19,000	3	65,001 - 70,000	11	17,001 - 22,000	3		
19,001 - 25,000	4	70,001 - 90,000	12	22,001 - 28,000	4		
25,001 - 32,000	5	90,001 - 105,000	13	28,001 - 40,000	5		
32,001 - 38,000	6	105,001 - 115,000	14	40,001 - 50,000	6		
38,001 - 42,000	7	115,001 and over	15	50,001 - 65,000	7		

Table 2: Two-Earner/Two-Job Worksheet

Married Filing Jointly		All Others	
If wages from **HIGHEST** paying job are—	Enter on line 7 above	If wages from **HIGHEST** paying job are—	Enter on line 7 above
$0 - $50,000	$440	$0 - $30,000	$440
50,001 - 100,000	800	30,001 - 60,000	800
100,001 - 130,000	900	60,001 - 120,000	900
130,001 - 250,000	1,000	120,001 - 270,000	1,000
250,001 and over	1,100	270,001 and over	1,100

U.S. Department of Justice
Immigration and Naturalization Service

OMB No. 1115-0136

Employment Eligibility Verification

Please read instructions carefully before completing this form. The instructions must be available during completion of this form. **ANTI-DISCRIMINATION NOTICE:** It is illegal to discriminate against work eligible individuals. Employers CANNOT specify which document(s) they will accept from an employee. The refusal to hire an individual because of a future expiration date may also constitute illegal discrimination.

Section 1. Employee Information and Verification. To be completed and signed by employee at the time employment begins.

Print Name: Last	First	Middle Initial	Maiden Name
Address (Street Name and Number)		Apt. #	Date of Birth (month/day/year)
City	State	Zip Code	Social Security #

I am aware that federal law provides for imprisonment and/or fines for false statements or use of false documents in connection with the completion of this form.	I attest, under penalty of perjury, that I am (check one of the following): ☐ A citizen or national of the United States ☐ A Lawful Permanent Resident (Alien # A_____) ☐ An alien authorized to work until ___/___/___ (Alien # or Admission #)_____
Employee's Signature	Date (month/day/year)

Preparer and/or Translator Certification. *(To be completed and signed if Section 1 is prepared by a person other than the employee.) I attest, under penalty of perjury, that I have assisted in the completion of this form and that to the best of my knowledge the information is true and correct.*

Preparer's/Translator's Signature	Print Name
Address (Street Name and Number, City, State, Zip Code)	Date (month/day/year)

Section 2. Employer Review and Verification. To be completed and signed by employer. Examine one document from List A OR examine one document from List B and one from List C, as listed on the reverse of this form, and record the title, number and expiration date, if any, of the document(s)

List A	OR	List B	AND	List C
Document title: _____		_____		_____
Issuing authority: _____		_____		_____
Document #: _____		_____		_____
Expiration Date (if any): ___/___/___		___/___/___		___/___/___
Document #: _____				
Expiration Date (if any): ___/___/___				

CERTIFICATION - I attest, under penalty of perjury, that I have examined the document(s) presented by the above-named employee, that the above-listed document(s) appear to be genuine and to relate to the employee named, that the employee began employment on *(month/day/year)* ___/___/___ and that to the best of my knowledge the employee is eligible to work in the United States. (State employment agencies may omit the date the employee began employment.)

Signature of Employer or Authorized Representative	Print Name	Title
Business or Organization Name	Address (Street Name and Number, City, State, Zip Code)	Date (month/day/year)

Section 3. Updating and Reverification. To be completed and signed by employer.

A. New Name (if applicable)	B. Date of rehire (month/day/year) (if applicable)

C. If employee's previous grant of work authorization has expired, provide the information below for the document that establishes current employment eligibility.

Document Title:_____ Document #:_____ Expiration Date (if any): ___/___/___

I attest, under penalty of perjury, that to the best of my knowledge, this employee is eligible to work in the United States, and if the employee presented document(s), the document(s) I have examined appear to be genuine and to relate to the individual.

Signature of Employer or Authorized Representative	Date (month/day/year)

Form I-9 (Rev. 11-21-91)N Page 2

You Have a Right to a Safe and Healthful Workplace.

IT'S THE LAW!

- You have the right to notify your employer or OSHA about workplace hazards. You may ask OSHA to keep your name confidential.
- You have the right to request an OSHA inspection if you believe that there are unsafe and unhealthful conditions in your workplace. You or your representative may participate in the inspection.
- You can file a complaint with OSHA within 30 days of discrimination by your employer for making safety and health complaints or for exercising your rights under the *OSH Act*.
- You have a right to see OSHA citations issued to your employer. Your employer must post the citations at or near the place of the alleged violation.
- Your employer must correct workplace hazards by the date indicated on the citation and must certify that these hazards have been reduced or eliminated.
- You have the right to copies of your medical records or records of your exposure to toxic and harmful substances or conditions.
- Your employer must post this notice in your workplace.

The *Occupational Safety and Health Act of 1970 (OSH Act)*, P.L. 91-596, assures safe and healthful working conditions for working men and women throughout the Nation. The Occupational Safety and Health Administration, in the U.S. Department of Labor, has the primary responsibility for administering the *OSH Act*. The rights listed here may vary depending on the particular circumstances. To file a complaint, report an emergency, or seek OSHA advice, assistance, or products, call 1-800-321-OSHA or your nearest OSHA office: • Atlanta (404) 562-2300 • Boston (617) 565-9860 • Chicago (312) 353-2220 • Dallas (214) 767-4731 • Denver (303) 844-1600 • Kansas City (816) 426-5861 • New York (212) 337-2378 • Philadelphia (215) 861-4900 • San Francisco (415) 975-4310 • Seattle (206) 553-5930. Teletypewriter (TTY) number is 1-877-889-5627. To file a complaint online or obtain more information on OSHA federal and state programs, visit OSHA's website at **www.osha.gov**. If your workplace is in a state operating under an OSHA-approved plan, your employer must post the required state equivalent of this poster.

1-800-321-OSHA
www.osha.gov

U.S. Department of Labor • Occupational Safety and Health Administration • OSHA 3165

Chapter 2

Accounting Forms

The purpose of this book is to present a simplified system of business recordkeeping that small business owners themselves can use to track their company's financial situation. The purpose of any business financial recordkeeping system is to provide a clear vision of the relative health of the business, both on a day-to-day basis and periodically. Business owners themselves need to know whether they are making a profit, why they are making a profit, which parts of the business are profitable and which are not. This information is only available if the business owner has a clear and straightforward recordkeeping system. Business owners also need to be able to produce accurate financial statements for income tax purposes, for loan proposals, and for the purpose of selling the business. The purpose of any business recordkeeping system is to allow the business owner to easily understand and use the information gathered. Certain accounting principles and terms have been adopted as standard over the years to make it easier to understand a wide range of business transactions. In order to understand what a recordkeeping system is trying to accomplish, it is necessary to define some of the standard ways of looking at a business.

The business recordkeeping system that is provided in this chapter will detail how to set up the books for a small business. The simplified small business accounting system which is provided is a modified single-entry accounting system. It is presented as a system for accrual-basis accounting for small businesses. The records are designed to be used on a calendar-year basis. Within these basic parameters, the system can be individually tailored to meet the needs of most small businesses. The purpose of a business financial recordkeeping system is to provide a method for the owner to keep track of the ongoing health of the business. This is done primarily by providing the owner with information on two basic financial statements: the balance sheet and the profit and loss statement.

Financial Recordkeeping Checklist

☐ Set up your business chart of accounts

☐ Open a business checking account

☐ Prepare a check register

☐ Set up a business petty cash fund

☐ Prepare a petty cash register

☐ Set up asset accounts

☐ Prepare current asset account records

☐ Prepare fixed asset account records

☐ Set up expense account records

☐ Set up income account records

☐ Set up payroll system

☐ Prepare payroll time sheets

☐ Prepare payroll depository records

☐ Determine proper tax forms for use in business

Chart of Accounts

The financial recordkeeping system that you will set up using this book is designed to be adaptable to any type of business. Whether your business is a service business, a manufacturing business, a retail business, a wholesale distributorship, or combination of any of these, you will be able to easily adapt this simplified system to work with your particular situation. A key to designing the most useful recordkeeping system for your particular needs is to examine your type of business in depth. After a close examination of the particular needs and operations of your type of business, you will need to set up an array of specific accounts to handle your financial records. This set of general accounts is called a *chart of accounts*.

A chart of accounts will list all of the various categories of financial transactions which you will need to track. There will be an account for each general type of expense which you want to keep track of. You will also have separate accounts for each type of income your business will receive. Accounts will also be set up for your business assets and liabilities. Setting up an account for each of these categories consists of the simple task of deciding which items you will need to categorize, selecting a name for the account, and assigning a number for the account.

Before you can set up your accounts, you need to understand the reason for setting up these separate accounts. It is possible, although definitely not recommended, to run a business and merely keep track of your income and expenses without any itemization at all. However, you would be unable to analyze how the business is performing beyond a simple check to see if you have any money left after paying the expenses. You would also be unable to properly fill in the necessary information for business income tax returns. A major reason for setting up separate accounts for many businesses expense and income transactions is to separate and itemize the amounts spent in each category so that this information is available at tax time. This insures that a business is taking all of its allowable business deductions. The main reason, however, to set up individual accounts is to allow the business owner to have a clear view of the financial health of the business. With separate accounts for each type of transaction, a business owner can analyze the proportional costs and revenues of each aspect of the business. Is advertising costing more than labor expenses? Is the income derived from sales items worth the discounts of the sale? Only by using the figures obtained from separate itemized accounts can these questions be answered.

In the following sections, you will select and number the various accounts for use in your business chart of accounts. You will select various income accounts, expense accounts, asset accounts, and liability accounts. For each account, you will also assign it a number. For ease of use, you should assign a particular number value to all accounts of one type. For example, all income accounts may be assigned numbers 10–29. Sales income may be Account Number 11; service income may be assigned Account Number 12, interest income may be Account Number 13. Similarly, expenses may be assigned numbers 30–79. Balance sheet accounts for assets and liabilities may be numbers 80–99. Be sure to leave enough numbers for future expansion of your list of accounts. Normally there will be far more expense accounts than any other type of account.

If you have income or expenses from many sources, you may wish to use three-digit numbers to identify each separate category. For example, if your business consists of renting out residential houses and you have ten properties, you may wish to set up a separate income and expense account for each property. You may wish to assign account numbers 110–119 to income from all properties. Thus, for example, you could then assign rental income from property number 1 to account number 111, rental income from property number 2 to account number 112, rental income from property number 3 to account number 113, and so on. Similarly, expenses can be broken down into separate accounts for individual properties. Advertising expenses might all be account numbers 510-519, thus advertising expenses for property number 1 might then be assigned number 511, advertising expenses for property number 2 would be assigned account number 512, etc.

How your individual chart of accounts will be organized will be specific to your particular business. If you have a simple business with all income coming from one source, you will probably desire a two-digit number from, perhaps, numbers 10–29 assigned to that income account. On the other hand, a more complex business with many sources of income and many different types of expenses may wish to use a system of three-digit numbers. Take some time to analyze your specific business to decide how you wish to set up your accounts. Ask yourself what type of information will you want to extract from your financial records. Do you need more details of your income sources? Then you should set up several income accounts for each type and possibly even each source of your income. Would you like more specific information on your expenses? Then you most likely would wish to set up clear and detailed expense accounts for each type of expense that you must pay.

Be aware that you may wish to alter your chart of accounts as your business grows. You may find that you have set up too many accounts and unnecessarily complicated your recordkeeping tasks. You may wish to set up more accounts once you see how your balance sheets and profit and loss statements look. You may change, add, or delete accounts at any time. Remember, however, that any transactions recorded in an account must be transferred to any new account or accounts that take the place of the old account.

Income Accounts

These are accounts that are used to track the various sources of your company's income. There may be only a few sources of income for your business, or you may wish to track your income in more detail. The information which you collect in your income accounts will be used to prepare your profit and loss statements periodically.

On the chart of accounts that is used in this book, income is separated into several categories. You can choose the income account categories which best suit your type of business. If your business is a service business, you may wish to set up accounts for labor income and for materials income. Or you may wish to set up income accounts in more detail, for example: sales income, markup income, income from separate properties, or income from separate sources in your business, etc. Non-sales income such as bank account interest income or income on the sale of business equipment should be placed in separate individual income accounts. Following is a list of various general income accounts. Decide how much detail you will want in your financial records regarding income and then choose the appropriate accounts. After you have chosen your income accounts, assign a number to each account.

Expense Accounts

These are the accounts that you will use to keep track of your expenses. Each separate category of expense should have its own account. Many of the types of accounts are dictated by the types of expenses which should be itemized for tax purposes. You will generally have separate accounts for advertising costs, utility expenses, rent, phone costs, etc. One or more separate accounts should also be set up to keep track of inventory expenses. These should be kept separate from other expense accounts as they must be itemized for tax purposes.

Following is a list of various general expense accounts. Please analyze your business and determine which accounts would be best suited to select for your particular situation. You will then number these accounts, as you did the income accounts. The categories presented are general categories that match most IRS forms. You may, of course, set up separate accounts that are not listed, to suit your particular needs.

INCOME CHART OF ACCOUNTS

Account Number	Account Name and Description
	Income from sale of goods
	Income from services
	Income from labor charges
	Income from sales discounts
	Income from interest revenue
	Income from consulting
	Miscellaneous income

EXPENSE CHART OF ACCOUNTS

Account Number	Account Name and Description
	Advertising expenses
	Auto expenses
	Cleaning and maintenance expenses
	Charitable contributions
	Dues and publications
	Office equipment expenses
	Freight and shipping expenses
	Business insurance expenses
	Business interest expenses
	Legal expenses
	Business meals and lodging
	Miscellaneous expenses
	Postage expenses
	Office rent expenses
	Repair expenses
	Office supplies
	Sales taxes paid
	Federal unemployment taxes paid
	State unemployment taxes paid
	Telephone expenses
	Utility expenses
	Wages and commissions

Asset and Liability Accounts

Asset and liability accounts are collectively referred to as *balance sheet accounts*. This is because the information collected on them is used to prepare your business Balance Sheets. You will set up current and fixed asset accounts and current and long-term liability accounts. Types of current asset accounts are cash, short-term notes receivable, accounts receivable, inventory, and prepaid expenses. Fixed assets may include equipment, vehicles, buildings, land, long-term notes receivable, and long-term loans receivable.

Types of current liability accounts are short-term notes payable (money due within one year), short-term loans payable (money due on a loan within one year), unpaid taxes, and unpaid wages. Long-term liability accounts may be long-term notes payable (money due more than one year in the future) or long-term loans payable (money due more than one year in the future). Finally, you will need an owner's equity account to tally the ownership value of your business. Choose the asset and liability accounts that best suit your business and assign appropriate numbers to each account.

BALANCE SHEET CHART OF ACCOUNTS

Account Number	Account Name and Description
	Accounts receivable (current asset)
	Bank checking account (current asset)
	Bank savings account (current asset)
	Cash on hand (current asset)
	Notes receivable (current asset, if short-term)
	Loans receivable (current asset, if short-term)
	Inventory (current asset)
	Land (fixed asset)
	Buildings (fixed asset)
	Vehicles (fixed asset)
	Equipment (fixed asset)
	Machinery (fixed asset)
	Accounts payable (current debt)
	Notes payable (current, if due within one year)
	Loans payable (current, if due within one year)
	Notes payable (long-term debt, if over one year)
	Loans payable (long-term debt, if over one year)
	Mortgage payable (long-term debt, if over one year)
	Owner's equity (if sole proprietorship)
	Partner's equity (if partnership)
	Retained capital (if corporation)

Business Bank Accounts and Petty Cash

The first financial action that a new small business should take is to set up a business bank account. A bank account is necessary to provide the business owner with a clear written record of all initial transactions. There are numerous types of business bank accounts available; some pay interest, some charge for each check written or deposited, some return your canceled checks each month, and some provide other benefits. Check with various local banking institutions to see which types are available and then choose the bank account which is best suited to your needs.

The business bank account will be the first record of many of your businesses' financial transactions. All of the income received by a business and all of the expenses that a business pays should be recorded in the check register for the business banking account. Your business bank account should always be a separate checking account. However, there may be instances when certain items will need to be paid for with cash. For this purpose, a *petty cash fund* will need to be set up. This is explained at the end of this section.

Bank Account Procedures

① Every transaction should be recorded in the check register. The details of each transaction will be important as you prepare your financial records.

② All of your business expenses and bills should be paid by check. If it is necessary to pay by cash, carefully record the payment in the Petty Cash Register which follows. Don't write checks to "Cash."

③ Balance your checking account every month. This is vital in keeping close track of your finances. If the bank's statement does not match your records, contact the bank to determine where the discrepancy is. Bouncing a check because you have insufficient funds in the bank will leave a blemish on the reputation of your business.

④ Never use your business bank account to pay for personal expenses. Keep all of your business finances scrupulously separate from your personal affairs. If some expenses are part personal and part business, make a careful record of the amount of each portion of the expense.

⑤ Retain your cancelled checks and bank statements for at least three years. If your business is ever audited by the Internal Revenue Service, you will need to produce these records to substantiate your business income and deductions.

In many respects, your business bank account is the main financial corridor for your business. In dealings with banks, suppliers, employees, and other businesses, your business account is the primary conduit for conducting your financial transactions. It is vital to your success that you are able to keep the records for this main financial account straight. On the next few pages, the following forms are provided to help you in this task: Check Register, Monthly Bank Statement Reconciliation Sheet, and a Petty Cash Register.

Check Register Instructions

1. The first transaction in the account will be the initial deposit. Put this on the first line in the register. Fill in the amount in the Deposit column. Carry this amount over into the Balance column.

2. If you desire, each transaction may take up two lines in the Register. The first line may be used to record the details of the transaction. The second line may be used to figure the balance. By using two lines, you will leave yourself enough room to allow for easy reading of the transactions.

3. For each check that is written, record the following information:
   - The date the check was written
   - The number of the check
   - The name of person or company that the check was written to
   - A description of the reason for the check (ie., what was purchased, what was paid for, etc.)
   - What expense account the check should be listed under. In the previous chapter, you set up Expense Account numbers for each type of expense. The appropriate account number should be entered in this column
   - The amount of the check

4. For each deposit, record the following information:
   - The date of the deposit
   - A description of the deposit. This should include information regarding what specific checks were deposited or if the deposit was cash
   - What Income Account number the deposit should be credited to
   - The amount of the deposit

5. For each transaction, the current balance of the checkbook should be calculated. This should be done at the time that you write the check or make the deposit. Don't let the balance go uncalculated for any length of time. Errors are more likely if you do not keep an accurate running balance.

CHECK REGISTER

Date	Number	Check Description	Number	Account Clear	Payment		Deposit		Balance	

Monthly Bank Statement Reconciliation

On the next page you will find a Monthly Bank Statement Reconciliation. Every month on this form, you will compare your bank statement with the balance in your Check Register. Using the method outlined will give you a clear picture of any discrepancies between the bank's records and your own. To fill in this form, follow these instructions:

① Fill in the month and year on the form. Fill in your account balance from your *bank statement* where shown. Fill in your account balance from your *check register* on the last line where shown.

② Using your check register, under Outstanding Checks on this form, fill in the amounts for each check that you have written that has not been checked off as "Clear." Total this amount and *subtract* it from the Bank Statement Balance where shown.

③ Again using your check register, under Outstanding Deposits on this form, fill in the amounts for any deposits that you have made that have not been checked off as "Clear." Total these deposits and *add* this amount to your Bank Statement Balance where shown.

④ If there are any service charges or other fees on your Bank Statement, total these and *subtract* them from the Bank Statement Balance where shown. If your account has earned any interest, *add* this to your Bank Statement Balance where shown.

⑤ Finish all of the calculations. The Final Balance shown on this sheet should match the balance shown on your Check Register. If it doesn't, go back over all of your calculations and try again. If it still doesn't match, carefully check your cancelled checks and deposits to make certain that you have checked off as "Clear" all of the appropriate items. If this does not rectify the error, you will need to check all of the amounts on all of the checks and deposits. This is often where the error was made. Check and recheck all of your calculations and entries. If you still cannot find the discrepancy, take your bank statement, check register, cancelled checks and deposit slips to your bank and ask them to check the balances. Most banks are more than willing to help their customers.

⑥ When you have finally reconciled your monthly statement with your check register, file the cancelled checks and bank statement. You will need to keep these bank records for at least three years.

MONTHLY BANK STATEMENT RECONCILIATION

Checks Outstanding			Deposits Outstanding		
Number	Amount		Date	Amount	
TOTAL			TOTAL		

Bank Statement Balance	
+ ADD Outstanding Deposits	
+ ADD Interest Earned	
= SUBTOTAL	
- SUBTRACT Outstanding Checks	
- SUBTRACT Service Charges/Fees	
= TOTAL *(This should agree with your Check Register Balance)*	

Petty Cash Register

The handling of cash often poses problems for small businesses. Unless you have a simple system to keep track of your petty cash in place, it is often difficult to keep accurate and current records of the use of cash in your business. The use of a petty cash fund provides you with a clear record of the payment of expenses with small amounts of cash; amounts that are too small to be handled by the use of a check. Petty cash is different from the cash which you might use in a cash register to take in payments for merchandise or services. For a petty cash fund, you generally will not need to set aside more than $50.00. Following is how to handle your petty cash:

① Get a small cash box or something similar, with a lock and key.

② Write a check from your business bank account made out to "Petty Cash" for the amount that you will begin your fund with. In your check register, record the account number as the account listed for your current asset account for cash on hand. Put the cash in the cash box.

③ Using the Petty Cash Register on the next page, record the starting amount as "Cash in," just like you would record a deposit in a checkbook register. Record cash that you pay out as "Cash out," similar to how you would record a payment in a check register.

④ Record each transaction that you make using your petty cash fund just as you would in a check register. Record the date, description of the use of the money or of money taken in, the account under which it should be listed, and the amount of the transaction.

⑤ When your petty cash fund gets low, note what the balance is and write another check to "Petty Cash" which will cause your balance to equal the amount that you have chosen as a total for your petty cash fund. For example, you have decided to have a $50.00 petty cash fund. In two months, you have used up $46.00 of the cash (and recorded each transaction). You should have $4.00 in cash left in your box and as a written balance on your Petty Cash Register. Simply write a check to "Petty Cash" for $46.00, cash the check, and put the cash in the box to replenish the petty cash fund.

⑥ At the time that you replenish your petty cash fund, you will need to record all of your transactions on your main income and expense record sheets. You will simply transfer all of the amounts to the main sheets and check the box on the petty cash ledger marking them as cleared transactions.

PETTY CASH REGISTER

Date	Description	Account Number	Clear	Cash Out		Cash In		Balance	

Business Assets and Inventory

After setting up a chart of accounts, a bank account, and a petty cash fund, the next financial recordkeeping task for a business will consist of preparing a method to keep track of the assets of the business. Recall that the assets of a business are everything that is owned by the business. They are either current assets that can be converted to cash within a year or fixed assets that are more long-term in nature. Each of these two main categories of assets will be discussed separately.

Current Assets

Following is a list of typical current assets for a business:

- Business bank checking account
- Business bank savings account
- Cash (petty cash fund and cash on hand)
- Accounts receivable (money owed to the company)
- Inventory

A company may have other types of current assets such as notes or loans receivable, but the five listed are the basic ones for most small businesses. In complex double-entry accounting systems, the current asset account balances are constantly being changed. In a double-entry system, each time an item of inventory is sold, for example, the account balance for the inventory account must be adjusted to reflect the sale. In the type of single-entry system that is presented in this book, all asset and liability accounts are updated only when the business owner wishes to prepare a balance sheet. This may be done monthly, quarterly, or annually. At a minimum, this updating must take place at the end of the year in order to have the necessary figures available for tax purposes. The forms and instructions in this book provide a simple method for tracking and updating the required information for business assets and liabilities.

The main form for tracking your current business assets will be a Current Asset Account sheet. A copy of this form follows this discussion. On this form, you will periodically track the value of the current asset that you are following, except for your inventory. (For inventory, you will use specialized inventory records.) You should prepare a separate Current Asset Account sheet for each asset. For example, if your current assets consist of a business checking account, cash on hand, and accounts receivable, you will have three separate Current Asset Accounts, one for each category of asset. These forms are very simple to use. Follow the instructions on the next page:

① Simply fill in the Account Number for the Current Asset Account for which you are setting up the form. You will get this number from your Chart of Accounts. Fill in also a description of the Account. For example: Account Number 53: Business Banking Account.

② You must then decide how often you will be preparing a balance sheet and updating your balance sheet account balances. If you wish to keep close track of your finances, you may wish to do this on a monthly basis. For many businesses, a quarterly balance sheet may be sufficient. All businesses, no matter how small, must prepare a balance sheet at least annually, at the end of the year. Decide how often you wish to update the balances and enter the period in the space provided.

③ Next, enter the date that you open the account. Under description, enter "Opening Balance." Under the "Balance" column, enter the opening value. The amount to enter for an opening balance will be as follows:
  + For a bank account this will be the opening balance of the account
  + For cash on hand, this will be the opening balance of the petty cash fund and cash on hand for sales, such as the cash used in a cash register.
  + For accounts receivable, this will be the total amount due from all accounts

④ Periodically, you will enter a date and new balance. You will enter these new balances from the following sources:
  + For bank accounts, this figure will come from your Check Register balance column on a particular date
  + For cash, this new figure will come from your Petty Cash Register balance and your Monthly Cash Report Summary on a certain date
  + For accounts receivable, the balance will come from your monthly Credit Sales Aging Report

⑤ After you have entered the balances on the appropriate Current Asset Account Sheet, you will transfer the balances to your Balance Sheet.

CURRENT ASSET ACCOUNT

Account No.:	Account Name:	Period:	
Date	Description of Asset	Balance	

Periodic Inventory Record

This is the form that you will use to keep continual track of your inventory if you have a relatively small inventory. You will use the Periodic Inventory Record for the purpose of keeping track of the costs of your inventory and of any orders of additional inventory. You will refer to this record when you need to order additional inventory, when you need to determine when an order should be received, and when you need to determine the cost of your inventory items at the end of the year, or at other times if desired. If you have an extensive inventory, you will need to consult an accounting professional to assist you in setting up a perpetual-type inventory system. Or you may be able to set up a complex inventory system using commercial accounting software that is available.

① Prepare a separate Periodic Inventory Record for each item of inventory. Identify the type of item that is being tracked by description and by item number, if applicable. You may also wish to list the supplier of the item.

② The first entry on the Periodic Inventory Record should be the initial purchase of inventory. On the right-hand side of the record, list the following items:
+ Date purchased
+ Quantity purchased
+ Price per item
+ Total price paid
+ Note: Shipping charges should not be included in the prices entered. Only the actual costs of the goods should be listed.

③ When you are running low on a particular item and place an order, on the left-hand side of the record enter the following information:
+ Date of the order
+ The order number
+ The quantity ordered
+ The date the order is due to arrive

④ When the order arrives, enter the actual details about the order on the right-hand side of the page. This will allow you to keep track of your order of inventory items and also allow you to keep track of the cost of your items of inventory.

PERIODIC INVENTORY RECORD

Item:				Item No:			
Supplier:							

Inventory Ordered				Inventory Received			
Date	Order No.	Quantity	Due	Date	Quantity	Price	Total

Perpetual Inventory Record

This is the form which you will use to keep continual track of your inventory if you have a relatively extensive inventory. You will refer to this record when you need to order additional inventory, determine when an order should be received, and determine the cost of your inventory items at the end of the year. Additionally, on this form you will keep track of the number of items of each type of inventory which have been sold.

① Prepare a separate Perpetual Inventory Record for each item of inventory. Identify the type of item which is being tracked by description and by item number, if applicable. You may also wish to list the supplier for the item.

② The first entry on the Perpetual Inventory Record should be the initial purchase of inventory. On the lower left-hand side of the record, under Inventory Received, list the following information:
  + Date purchased
  + Quantity purchased
  + Price per item
  + Total price paid
  + Note: Shipping charges should not be included in the amounts entered

③ When you are running low on a particular item and place an order, on the upper left-hand side of the record enter the following information:
  + Date of the order
  + Order number
  + Quantity ordered
  + The date the ordered inventory is due

④ When the order arrives, enter the actual details on the lower left-hand side of the page, under Inventory Received.

⑤ On the right-hand side of the record, keep a running total of the number of items of inventory sold. Decide how often you will be checking your stocks to update your inventory counts and stick to the schedule: weekly, monthly, or quarterly. Enter the number of items sold at each count and figure the totals. This will give you a running total of the amount of inventory you have in stock at any given time. You will, however, still need to take a physical inventory count at the end of the year (or more often) to check for lost, stolen, miscounted, or missing items and as a check against your calculations.

PERPETUAL INVENTORY RECORD

Item: Item No.:

Supplier:

Inventory Ordered				Inventory in Stock				
Date	Order No.	Quantity	Due	Date	Quantity	Price		Total	

Inventory Received			
Date	Quantity	Price	Total

Physical Inventory Record

This form should be used to record the results of an actual physical counting of the inventory at the end of the year and at whatever other times during the year you decide to take a physical inventory. If you decide that you will need to track your inventory monthly or quarterly, you may need to prepare this form for those time periods. To prepare this form, take the following steps:

① The form should be dated and signed by the person doing the inventory.

② The quantity and description of each item of inventory should be listed, along with an item number if applicable.

③ The cost (to you) of each item then should be listed under "Unit Price." A total per-item cost is then calculated by multiplying the quantity of units times the unit price. This total per-item cost should be listed in the far right-hand column. You will need to extract this per-item unit price from your Periodic or Perpetual Inventory forms.

④ The total inventory cost should be figured by adding all of the figures in the far right-hand column.

PHYSICAL INVENTORY RECORD

Date:	Taken by:				
Quantity	Description	Item No.	Unit Price		Total	
				TOTAL		

Cost of Goods Sold Record

The final record for inventory control is the *Cost of Goods Sold Record*. It is on this record that you will determine the actual cost to your business of the goods which were sold during a particular time period. There are numerous methods to determine the value of your inventory at the end of a time period. The three most important are the Specific Identification method, the first-in first-out method (called FIFO) and the last-in first-out method (called LIFO).

Specific Identification is the easiest to use if you have only a few items of inventory, or one-of-a-kind types of merchandise. With this method, you actually keep track of each specific item of inventory. You keep track of when you obtained the item, its cost, and when you sold the specific item.

With the FIFO method, you keep track only of general quantities of your inventory. Your inventory costs are calculated as though the oldest inventory merchandise was sold first: The first items that you purchased are the first items that you sell.

With the LIFO method, the cost values are calculated as though you sell your most-recently purchased inventory first. It is important to note that you do not necessarily have to actually sell your first item first to use the FIFO method and you do not have to actually sell your last item first to use the LIFO method of calculation.

Although there may be significant advantages in some cases to using the LIFO method, it is also a far more complicated system than the FIFO. The Specific Identification allows you to simply track each item of inventory and deduct the actual cost of the goods which you sold during the year. The FIFO method allows you to value your inventory on hand at the end of a time period based on the cost of your most recent purchases. Using either your Periodic or Perpetual Inventory Records, valuing your inventory is a simple matter.

① At the end of your chosen time period (monthly, quarterly, or annually), take an actual physical inventory count on your Physical Inventory Record.

② Using the most recent purchases as listed on your Periodic or Perpetual Inventory Record, determine the unit price of the items left in your inventory and enter this under the Unit Price column on your Physical Inventory Record.

③ Once all of your items of inventory have been checked, counted, and a unit price determined, simply total each item and then total the value of the entire inventory. If you are conducting your final annual inventory, this final figure is your Inventory value at year end.

④ On the Cost of Goods Sold Record, enter this number on the line titled: Inventory Value at End of Period. If this is your first year in business, enter zero as the Inventory Value at Beginning of Period. For later periods, the Inventory Value at Beginning of Period will be the Inventory Value at End of Period for the previous period.

⑤ Using either your Periodic Inventory or your Perpetual Inventory Record sheets, total the amounts of orders during the period which are listed under the Inventory Received column. This total will be entered on the Inventory Added During Period line. Now simply perform the calculations. You will use the figures on this sheet at tax time to prepare your taxes.

NOTE: This type of inventory calculation is not intended for manufacturing companies that manufacture finished goods from raw materials or for those with gross annual receipts over $10 million. For those type of companies, an additional calculation is necessary because of uniform capitalization rules. This tax rule requires that manufacturing inventory values include the overhead associated with the manufacturing process. Please consult an accounting professional if you fall into this category of business.

COST OF GOODS SOLD RECORD

Period Ending:

Inventory Value at Beginning of Period	
Plus Inventory Added During Period	
Equals Total Inventory Value	
Less Inventory Value at End of Period	
Equals Cost of Goods Sold	
Beginning Inventory Value for Next Period	

Fixed Asset Account

Recall that fixed assets are business purchases that are depreciable, unless you elect to deduct fixed asset expenses up to $20,000.00 per year. For recordkeeping purposes, you will prepare a Fixed Asset Account record for each fixed asset that you have if you have acquired more than $20,000.00 in a calendar year. If you have acquired less than $20,000.00 worth in a year, you may put all of your fixed asset records on one Fixed Asset Account record.

To prepare your Fixed Asset Account record, follow these instructions:

① List the date on which you acquired the property. If the property was formerly personal property, list the date on which you converted it to business property.

② Then list the property by description. Enter the actual cost of the property. If the property is used, enter the lower amount of the cost of the property or the actual market value of the property. If the property is part business and part personal, enter the value of the business portion of the property.

③ If you will have more than $20,000.00 worth of depreciable business property during the year, you additionally will need to enter information in the last three columns on the record. First, you will need to enter the recovery period for each asset. For most property other than buildings, this will be either five or seven years. Please consult a tax manual or tax professional.

④ You will need to enter the method of depreciation. Again, check a tax manual or tax professional.

⑤ Finally, you will need to determine the amount of the deduction for the first year (*Hint:* tax manual or tax professional).

⑥ Once you have set up a method for each fixed asset, each year you will determine the additional deduction and update the balance. You will then use that figure on your business tax return and in the preparation of your Balance Sheet.

FIXED ASSET ACCOUNT

Date	Item	Cost		Years	Method	Annual	Balance	

Business Debts

Business debts are also referred to as *business liabilities*. However, technically, business liabilities also include the value of the owner's equity in the business.

Business debts can be divided into two general categories. First are current debts, those that normally will be paid within one year. The second general category is long-term debts. Generally, these are more long-term debts or those that will not be paid off within one year. Current debts for most small businesses consist primarily of accounts payable and taxes that are due during the year. For small businesses, the taxes that are due during a year fall into three main categories: estimated income tax payments, payment of collected sales taxes, and payroll taxes. Since the collection and payment of sales taxes are handled differently in virtually every state, you will need to contact your state's department of revenue or similar body to determine the specific necessary record-keeping requirements for that business debt.

That leaves us with only accounts payable to track as a current debt. You will have only one simple form to use to keep track of this important category. Accounts payable are the current bills that your business owes. They may be for equipment or supplies that you have purchased on credit or they may be for items that you have ordered on account. Regardless of the source of the debt, you will need a clear system to record the debt and keep track of how much you still owe on the debt.

Long-term debts of a business are those debts that will not be paid off within one year. These are, generally, debts based on business loans for equipment, inventory, business-owned vehicles, or business property. In the accounting system outlined in this book, you will only keep track of the current principal and interest for these debts. For long-term debts of your business, you will fill in the *Long-Term Debt Record*, explained later in this chapter.

On the following page, you will find an *Accounts Payable Record*. If you have only a few accounts which you do not pay off immediately, you can use this form. If you have many accounts payable, you will need to complete an *Individual Account Payable Record* for each separate account. That form and its instructions immediately follow the Accounts Payable Record.

Accounts Payable Record

On the following form, you will enter any bills or short-term debts that you do not pay immediately. If you pay the bill off upon receipt of the bill, you need not enter the amount on this record. Your records for expenses will take care of the necessary documentation for those particular debts. If your business has many accounts payable that must be tracked, it may be a good idea to prepare an individual Accounts Payable Record for each account.

Follow these instructions to prepare and fill in this particular form:

① For those debts that you do not pay off immediately, in the left-hand column of the record, you will need to record the following information:
   + The date the debt was incurred
   + To whom you owe the money
   + Payment terms (for instance: due within 30, 60, or 90 days)
   + The amount of the debt

② In the right-hand column of the Accounts Payable Record, you will record the following information:
   + The date of any payments
   + To whom the payments were made
   + The amount of any payments made

③ By periodically totaling the left- and right-hand columns, you will be able to take a look at the total amount of your unpaid accounts payable. You may wish to do this weekly, monthly, or quarterly. You will also need the figure for your total unpaid accounts payable for the preparation of your Balance Sheet.

④ When you have totaled your accounts payable at the end of your chosen periodic interval, you should start a new record and carry the unpaid accounts over to it. Using this simple record, you will be able to check your accounts payable at a glance and also have enough information available to use to prepare a Balance Sheet for your business.

ACCOUNTS PAYABLE RECORD

Period from: to:

Unpaid Accounts					Payments			
Date	Due To	Terms	Amount		Date	Paid To	Amount	
		TOTAL					TOTAL	

TOTAL Unpaid Accounts

\- TOTAL Payments

\= TOTAL Accounts Payable

Individual Accounts Payable Record

If your business has many accounts payable which must be tracked, it may be a good idea to prepare an Individual Accounts Payable Record for each account. On the following page, you will find an Individual Accounts Payable Record to be used for this purpose. In order to fill in this record, follow these directions:

1. You will need to enter the following information for each account to whom a bill is owed:
   - Name
   - Address
   - Contact person
   - Phone number
   - An account number, if applicable

2. As you receive a bill or invoice, enter the following information off the bill or invoice:
   - Date
   - Invoice number
   - Any terms
   - Amount due

3. When an amount is paid, enter this information:
   - Check number
   - Date paid
   - Amount paid

4. Total the balance due after each transaction. Using this method of tracking accounts payable will allow you to always have a running total of your individual accounts payable available.

5. To prepare a balance sheet entry for accounts payable, you will simply need to total all of the various account balances for all of your accounts payable.

INDIVIDUAL ACCOUNTS PAYABLE RECORD

Company:

Address:

Contact Person: Phone:

Account Number: Interest Rate:

Date	Invoice/Check	Terms	Amount		Balance	

Long-Term Debt Record

If your business has any outstanding loans that will not be paid off within one year, you will prepare a *Long-Term Debt Record* for each loan. You will track the principal and interest paid on each long-term debt of your business. This information will enable you to have long-term debt figures for use in preparing your Balance Sheet and interest paid figures for use in preparing your Profit and Loss Statements. On the following page, you will find a record to be used for this purpose. In order to fill in this record, follow these directions:

① You will need to enter the following information for each company to whom a loan is outstanding:
  + Name
  + Address
  + Contact person
  + Phone number
  + Loan account number
  + Loan interest rate
  + Original principal amount of the loan
  + Term of the loan

② You will need a loan payment book or amortization schedule in order to obtain the necessary information regarding the portions of each of your payments that are principal and interest. As you make a payment, enter the following information:
  + Date of payment
  + Amount of principal paid
  + Amount of interest paid
  + Balance due (previous balance minus payment)

③ Total the balance due after each payment. Using this method of tracking accounts payable will allow you to always have a running total of your long-term liability for each long-term debt.

④ To prepare a Balance Sheet entry for long-term debts, you will simply need to total all of the various account balances for all of your long-term debts.

⑤ You should also periodically total all of the columns on your Long-Term Debt Record. You will need the totals for interest paid for your Annual Expense Summary.

LONG-TERM DEBT RECORD

Company:

Address:

Contact Person: Phone:

Account Number: Interest Rate:

Original Loan Amount: Term:

Date	Payment		Principal		Interest		Balance	
TOTAL								

Business Expenses

The expenses of a business are all of the transactions of the business in which money is paid out of the business, with two general exceptions. Money paid out of the business to the owner (as a draw rather than as a salary) and money paid out of the business to pay off the principal of a loan are not considered expenses of a business. Very often, the bulk of a small businesses' recordkeeping will consist of tracking its expenses. Because of the tax deductibility of the cost of most business expenses, it is crucial for a business to keep careful records of what has been spent to operate the business. But even beyond the need for detailed expense records for tax purposes, a small business needs a clear system which will allow for a quick examination of where business money is being spent. The tracking of business expenses will allow you to see at a glance where your money is flowing. With detailed records, it will also be an easy task to apply various financial formulas to analyze and understand your expense/income ratios in greater depth. This will allow you to see if certain costs are out-of-line, if certain expenses are increasing or decreasing, and if your business expenses make clear business sense.

In order to track your business expenses, you will use two main forms, either a Daily or a Weekly Expense Record (depending on the volume of your business expenses) and a Monthly Expense Record Summary. You may also need to use a number of additional specialized forms if your business needs dictate their use. The specialized forms which are included will cover the additional recordkeeping necessary to document travel expenses, meals and entertainment expenses, and vehicle expenses. There is also a Quarterly and Annual Expense Record Summary for totaling your expense payments.

Tracking Expenses

All of your expenses will initially be recorded on either the Daily or Weekly Expense Record sheet. You will have to choose if you desire to track your expenses on a daily form or a weekly form. If you anticipate having a great number of entries, choose a daily sheet for recording the expenses. If your expense transactions will generally number under 30 per week, you can use the weekly record. Regardless of which time period you choose to have on each sheet, you should record the expenditures at least weekly so that you do not fall too far behind in keeping it up-to-date. You may switch between recording periods if your level of expenses changes.

On your expense record sheet, you will record all of your business expenses in chronological order. The expense transactions will generally come from two main sources: your business bank account check register and your petty cash register. You will transfer all of the expenses from these two sources to the main expense record sheets. This will provide you with a central listing of all of the expenditures for your business.

From this record sheet (whether it is a daily or weekly record), you will transfer your expenses to a Monthly Expense Record. On the Monthly Expense Record sheet, you will enter a line for each expense type which you have listed on your business Chart of Accounts. You will then go through your Daily or Weekly Expense Record sheets for each month and total the expenses for each account. You will enter this total in the column for the specific type of expense.

Finally, on a monthly basis, you will transfer the totals for your various expense categories to the Annual Expense Summary sheet. On this sheet, you collect and record the total monthly expenses. With these figures, you will be able to easily total your expense amounts to ascertain your quarterly and annual expenses.

By recording your business expenses in this manner, you should have little difficulty being able to keep track of the money flowing out of your business on a daily, weekly, monthly, quarterly, and annual basis. You will have all of the information you will need to easily provide the necessary expenditure figures for preparing a Profit and Loss Statement.

On the next few pages are detailed explanations of how to fill in these various simplified forms. Remember that you must tailor the forms to fit your particular business.

Daily and Weekly Expense Records

On the following pages are both the Daily Expense Record and Weekly Expense Record forms. These forms are identical except for the period which they are intended to cover.

① Decide which time period you wish to use for completing the forms. If you anticipate over 30 expense transactions a week, you should probably choose the Daily Expense Record. Otherwise, the Weekly Expense Record should be sufficient.

② Fill in the date or dates which the form will cover at the top where indicated.

③ Beginning with your Bank Account Check Register, transfer the following in formation from the register to the Expense Record:
   + The date of the transaction
   + The check number
   + To whom the amount was paid
   + The expense account number (off your Chart of Accounts)
   + The amount of the transaction

86

④ Next, using your Petty Cash Register, transfer the following information from your Petty Cash Register to the Expense Record:
   + The date of the transaction
   + In the column for Check Number, put PC to indicate that the expense was a petty cash expense
   + To whom the amount was paid
   + The expense account number (off your Chart of Accounts)
   + The amount of the transaction
   + Do not list the checks that you make out to "Petty Cash" as an expense

⑤ For credit card transactions, follow these rules:
   + Do not list the payment to a credit card company as an expense
   + List the monthly amount on the credit card bill for interest as an interest expense
   + Individually, list each of the business purchases on the credit card as a separate expense item, assigning an account number to each separate business charge. Make a notation for the date, to whom the expense was paid, and the amount. In the column for Check Number, provide the type of credit card (for example: V for Visa)
   + Do not list any personal charge items as business expenses
   + If a charged item is used partially for business and partially for personal reasons, list only that portion which is used for business reasons as a business expense

⑥ At the end of the period (daily or weekly), total the Amount column. You will use this daily or weekly total expense amount to cross check your later calculations.

⑦ It is a good idea to keep all of your various business expense receipts for at least three years after the tax period to which they relate. You may wish to buy envelopes for each weekly period, label each appropriately, and file your weekly business expense receipts in them. This will make it easy to find each specific receipt, if necessary.

Monthly Expense Record

Using this record, you will compile and transfer the total expense amount for each expense category. In this way, you will be able to keep a monthly total of all of the expenses, broken down by category of expense. To fill in this form, do the following:

① Indicate the month that the Record will cover where shown at the top.

② In the first column on the left-hand side, list all of your expense account numbers from your business Chart of Accounts.

③ In the next column, using your Daily or Weekly Expense Records, transfer the amounts for each expense. If you have more than four expense amounts for any account, use a second Monthly Expense Record to record additional amounts.

④ In the Total column, list the total expenses in each category for the month.

⑤ At the bottom of the page, total the amount for all of the categories for the month. Don't forget to include any amounts from any additional records in your totals.

⑥ To double-check your transfers and your calculations, total all of your Daily or Weekly Expense Record total amounts. This figure should equal your Monthly Expense Record total for that month. If there is a discrepancy, check each of your figures until you discover the error.

Annual Expense Summary

① Fill in the year. Fill in your account numbers from your Chart of Accounts across the top row. If you have more than nine expense accounts, use a second and third page, if necessary.

② On a monthly basis, carry the totals from all of the rows on your Monthly Expense Records to the appropriate column of the Annual Expense Summary.

③ At the end of each quarter, total all of the monthly entries to arrive at your quarterly totals for each category.

④ To double-check your monthly calculations, total your categories across each month and put this total in the final column. Compare this total with the total on your Monthly Expense Records. If there is a discrepancy, check each of your figures until you discover the error. Don't forget to include your extra records if you have more than nine expense accounts to list.

⑤ To double-check your quarterly calculations, total your monthly totals in the final quarterly column. This figure should equal the total of the quarterly category totals across the quarterly row. If there is a discrepancy, check each of your figures until you discover the error.

⑥ Finally, total each of your quarterly amounts to arrive at the annual totals. To cross-check your calculations, total the quarterly totals in the final column. This figure should equal the total for all of the annual totals in each category across the Annual Total row. If there is a discrepancy, check each of your figures until you discover the error.

DAILY EXPENSE RECORD

Week of:

Date	Check No.	To Whom Paid	Account	Amount	
			Daily TOTAL		

WEEKLY EXPENSE RECORD

Week of:

Date	Check No.	To Whom Paid	Account	Amount	
			Weekly TOTAL		

MONTHLY EXPENSE RECORD

Account Name	Amount		Amount		Amount		Amount		Total	
								TOTAL		

ANNUAL EXPENSE SUMMARY

Year of:											
Account No.											Total
January											
February											
March											
1st Quarter											
April											
May											
June											
2nd Quarter											
July											
August											
September											
3rd Quarter											
October											
November											
December											
4th Quarter											
Annual TOTAL											

Weekly or Monthly Travel Expense Records

① Decide whether you will need to track your travel expenses on a weekly or monthly basis. For most businesses a monthly record will be adequate.

② Fill in the time period and the employee name.

③ For each separate expense, fill in the date and a description of the item. Place the amount for the item in the appropriate column (Travel, Lodging, Meals, or Other). Carry the amount over to the Total column.

④ At the end of the month (or week if you are keeping records on a weekly basis), total each column in the final Total row. To check for accuracy, the totals of the Travel, Lodging, Meals, and Other columns should equal the total for the Total column.

Annual Travel Expense Summary

① Fill in the year and employee name.

② On a monthly basis, carry the totals from all of the columns on your Weekly or Monthly Travel Expense Record forms to the appropriate column of the Annual Travel Expense Summary form.

③ At the end of each quarter, total all of the monthly entries to arrive at your quarterly totals for each category.

④ To double-check your monthly calculations, total your categories across each month and put this total in the final column. Compare this total with the total on your Weekly or Monthly Travel Expense Record sheets. If there is a discrepancy, check each of your figures until you discover the error.

⑤ To double-check your quarterly calculations, total your monthly totals in the final quarterly column. This figure should equal the total of the quarterly category totals across the quarterly row. If there is a discrepancy, check each of your figures until you discover the error.

⑥ Finally, total each of your quarterly amounts to arrive at the annual totals. To cross-check your calculations, total the quarterly totals in the final column. This figure should equal the total for all of the annual totals in each category across the Annual Totals row. If there is a discrepancy, check each of your figures until you discover the error

WEEKLY TRAVEL EXPENSE RECORD

Week of: Employee Name:

Date	Item	Travel		Lodging		Meals		Other		Other	
	Weekly TOTAL										

MONTHLY TRAVEL EXPENSE RECORD

Date	Item	Travel	Lodging	Meals	Other	Other
	Monthly TOTAL					

Month of: Employee Name:

ANNUAL TRAVEL EXPENSE SUMMARY

Year of: Employee Name:

Date	Item	Travel	Lodging	Meals	Other	Total
January						
February						
March						
1st Quarter						
April						
May						
June						
2nd Quarter						
July						
August						
September						
3rd Quarter						
October						
November						
December						
4th Quarter						
	Annual TOTAL					

Weekly or Monthly Auto Expense Records

① Decide whether you will need to track your auto expenses on a weekly or monthly basis. For most businesses a monthly record will be adequate.

② Fill in the time period, the employee name, car make and model, and license number.

③ For each separate expense, fill in the date and a description of the item. Place the amount for the item in the appropriate column (Gas/Oil or Other). Carry the amount over to the Total column. List the mileage driven for the period.

④ At the end of the month (or week if you are keeping records on a weekly basis), total each column in the final Weekly or Monthly Totals row. To check for accuracy, the totals of the Gas/Oil and Other columns should equal the total for the Total column.

Annual Auto Expense Summary

① Fill in the year, employee name, car make and model, and license number.

② On a monthly basis, carry the totals from all of the columns on your Weekly or Monthly Auto Expense Record forms to the appropriate column of the Annual Auto Expense Summary form.

③ At the end of each quarter, total all of the monthly entries to arrive at your quarterly totals for each category.

④ To double-check your monthly calculations, total your categories across each month and put this total in the final column. Compare this total with the total on your Weekly or Monthly Auto Expense Record sheets. If there is a discrepancy, check each of your figures until you discover the error.

⑤ To double-check your quarterly calculations, total your monthly totals in the final quarterly column. This figure should equal the total of the quarterly category totals across the quarterly row. If there is a discrepancy, check each of your figures until you discover the error.

⑥ Finally, total each of your quarterly amounts to arrive at the annual totals. To cross-check your calculations, total the quarterly totals in the final column. This figure should equal the total for all of the annual totals in each category across the Annual Totals row. If there is a discrepancy, check each of your figures until you discover the error.

WEEKLY AUTO EXPENSE RECORD

Week of:		Employee Name:			
Car Make/Model:		License Number:			

Date	Description	Mileage	Gas/Oil	Other	Total
	Weekly TOTAL				

MONTHLY AUTO EXPENSE RECORD

Week of: Employee Name:

Car Make/Model: License Number:

Date	Description	Mileage	Gas/Oil		Other		Total	
		Monthly TOTAL						

ANNUAL AUTO EXPENSE SUMMARY

Week of:		Employee Name:			
Car Make/Model:		License Number:			
Date	Description	Mileage	Gas/Oil	Other	Total
January					
February					
March					
1st Quarter					
April					
May					
June					
2nd Quarter					
July					
August					
September					
3rd Quarter					
October					
November					
December					
4th Quarter					
	Annual TOTAL				

Weekly or Monthly Meals and Entertainment Expense Records

① Decide whether you will need to track your meals and entertainment expenses on a weekly or monthly basis. For most businesses a monthly record will be adequate.

② Fill in the time period and the employee name.

③ For each separate expense, fill in the date, description of the item, and business purpose. Place the amount for the item in the appropriate column (Meals or Entertainment). Carry the amount over to the Total column.

④ At the end of the month (or week if you are keeping records on a weekly basis), total each column in the final Weekly or Monthly Totals row. To check for accuracy, the totals of the Meals and Entertainment columns should equal the total for the Total column.

Annual Meals and Entertainment Expense Summary

① Fill in the year and employee name.

② On a monthly basis, carry the totals from all of the columns on your Weekly or Monthly Meals and Entertainment Expense Record forms to the appropriate column of the Annual Meals and Entertainment Expense Summary form.

③ At the end of each quarter, total all of the monthly entries to arrive at your quarterly totals for each category.

④ To double-check your monthly calculations, total your categories across each month and put this total in the final column. Compare this total with the total on your Weekly or Monthly Meals and Entertainment Expense Record sheets. If there is a discrepancy, check each of your figures until you discover the error.

⑤ To double-check your quarterly calculations, total your monthly totals in the final quarterly column. This figure should equal the total of the quarterly category totals across the quarterly row. If there is a discrepancy, check each of your figures until you discover the error.

⑥ Finally, total each of your quarterly amounts to arrive at the annual totals. To cross-check your calculations, total the quarterly totals in the final column. This figure should equal the total for all of the annual totals in each category across the Annual Totals row. If there is a discrepancy, check each of your figures until you discover the error.

WEEKLY MEALS AND ENTERTAINMENT EXPENSE RECORD

Week of: _____ Employee Name: _____

Date	Item	Business Purpose	Meals		Entertainment		Total	
		Weekly TOTAL						

I confirm that the information on this form is true and correct, and that all of the expenses are business-related. All receipts are attached to this form.

_____   _____
Signature   Date

MONTHLY MEALS AND ENTERTAINMENT EXPENSE RECORD

Month of: Employee Name:

Date	Item	Business Purpose	Meals		Entertainment		Total	
		Monthly TOTAL						

I confirm that the information on this form is true and correct, and that all of the expenses are business-related. All receipts are attached to this form.

_____   _____

Signature   Date

ANNUAL MEALS AND ENTERTAINMENT EXPENSE SUMMARY

Year of:	Employee Name:						
Date	Item	Meals		Entertainment		Total	
January							
February							
March							
1st Quarter							
April							
May							
June							
2nd Quarter							
July							
August							
September							
3rd Quarter							
October							
November							
December							
4th Quarter							
	Annual TOTAL						

Purchase Order

Two final forms which may be used for business expenses are the Purchase Order and the Purchase Order Record. A Purchase Order is used for placing orders for business merchandise when a credit account has been established with a company in advance. You should use the following Purchase Order in conjunction with the Purchase Order Record which follows. Your Purchase Order Record provides you with a simple record of what you have ordered using your Purchase Orders.

① Place your business card in the upper left-hand corner of the blank Purchase Order form from this book and make a master copy on a copy machine. Make a number of copies of the master copy of your Purchase Order. Number your Purchase Orders consecutively.

② Using your first numbered Purchase Order, enter the date. Under Ship Via, enter how you wish the order to be shipped to you (ie., UPS ground, US Mail, Freight Carrier, etc.).

③ If you have a delivery deadline date, enter under Deliver By:.

④ Enter the appropriate information under Bill To: and Ship To:.

⑤ For each item ordered enter the following:
   ✦ Item Number
   ✦ Quantity
   ✦ Description
   ✦ Price and Amount

⑥ Subtotal and add tax and shipping if you know the correct amounts. Check the appropriate box under Terms.

⑦ Upon completing each Purchase Order, enter the following information on your Purchase Order Record:
   ✦ Purchase Order Number
   ✦ Date
   ✦ Vendor name
   ✦ Brief description of what was ordered
   ✦ Date when due
   ✦ Amount of the purchase order

105

PURCHASE ORDER

Date:

Purchase Order No.:

Ship via:

Deliver by:

Ship to:

Bill to:

Item No.	Quantity	Description	Price		Amount	

TERMS

❏ Cash
❏ COD
❏ On Account
❏ MC/VISA

Subtotal

Tax

Shipping

TOTAL

PURCHASE ORDER RECORD

P.O. No.	Date	Issued to	For	Due	Amount	

Business Income

The careful tracking of your business income is one of the most important accounting activities you will perform. It is essential for your business that you know intimately where your income comes from. Failure to accurately track income and cash is one of the most frequent causes of business failure. You must have in place a clear and easily-understood system to track your business income. There are three separate features of tracking business income that must be incorporated into your accounting system. You will need a system in place to handle cash, a system to track all of your sales and service income, and a system to handle credit sales.

The first system you will need is a clear method for handling cash on a daily or weekly basis. This is true no matter how large or small your business may be and regardless of how much or how little cash is actually handled. You must have a clear record of how much cash is on hand and of how much cash is taken in during a particular time period. You will also need to have a method to tally this cash flow on a monthly basis. For these purposes, three forms are provided: a Daily or Weekly Cash Report and a Monthly Cash Report Summary.

The second feature of your business income tracking system should be a method to track your actual income from sales or services. This differs from your cash tracking. With these records you will track taxable and nontaxable income whether the income is in the form of cash, check, credit card payment, or on account. Please note that when *nontaxable income* is referred to, it means only income that is not subject to any state or local sales tax (generally, this will be income from the performance of a service). These records will also track your intake of sales taxes, if applicable. For this segment of your income tracking, you will have either a Daily or Weekly Income Record. You will also track your income on Monthly Income Summaries that will provide you with a monthly, quarterly, and annual report of your taxable income, nontaxable income, and sales tax collection.

The third feature of your business income tracking consists of a method to track and bill credit sales. With this portion of income tracking, you will list and track all of your sales to customers that are made on account or on credit. The accounts that owe you money are referred to as your *accounts receivable*. They are the accounts from whom you hope to receive payment. The tracking of these credit sales will take place on a Daily, Weekly, or Monthly Credit Sales Record. You will also use a Credit Sales Aging Report to see how your customers are doing over time. The actual billing of these credit sales will require you to prepare and incorporate an Invoice, Statement, and Past Due Statement. Finally, a Credit Memo will be used to track those instances when a customer is given credit for any returned items.

Tracking Cash

Most businesses will have to handle cash in some form. Here we are not talking about the use of petty cash. Petty cash is the cash that a business has on hand for the payment of minor expenses that may crop up and for which the use of a business check is not convenient. The cash handling discussed in this section is the daily handling of cash used to take in money from customers or clients and the use of a cash drawer or some equivalent. You must have some method to accurately account for the cash used in your business in this regard. Three forms are provided: a Daily or Weekly Cash Report and a Monthly Cash Report Summary. The use of these forms is explained on the next pages.

Daily or Weekly Cash Report

This form is used each day or week to track the cash received in the business from customer payments to the business, not petty cash. The cash may be in a cash box, or some type of cash register. Regardless of how your cash is held, you need a method to account for the cash. Please follow these instructions:

① First, you will need to decide if you wish to track your cash transactions on a daily or weekly basis. Depending on the level of your business, choose to use either a Daily or Weekly Cash Report.

② You must decide how much cash you will need to begin each period with sufficient cash to meet your needs and make change for cash sales. Usually $100.00 should be sufficient for most needs. Choose a figure and begin each period with that amount in your cash drawer. Excess cash that has been collected should be deposited in your business bank account. Each period, fill in the date and the cash on hand on your Cash Report.

③ As you take in cash and checks throughout the period, record each item of cash taken in, checks taken in, and any instances of cash paid out. Cash out does not mean change that has been made, but rather cash paid out for business purposes (for example, a refund).

④ Your business may have so much daily cash flow that it will be burdensome to record each item of cash flow on your sheet. In that case, you will need a cash register of some type. Simply total the cash register at the end of the day and record the total cash in, checks in, and cash out in the appropriate places on the Daily Cash Report.

⑤ At the end of each period, total your Cash In and Checks In. Add these two amounts to your Cash on Hand at the beginning of the period. This equals your Total Receipts for the period. Subtract any Cash Out from this amount. This figure should equal your actual cash on hand at the end of the period. Make a bank deposit for all of the checks and for all of the cash in excess of the amount that you will need to begin the next period.

⑥ In the space for deposits, note the following: a deposit number, if applicable; the date of the deposit; the deposit amount; and the name and signature of the person who made the deposit. Don't forget to also record your deposit in your business Bank Account Check Register.

Monthly Cash Report Summary

This form will be used to keep a monthly record of your Daily or Weekly Cash Reports. It serves as a monthly listing of your cash flow and of your business bank account deposits. You will, of course, also record your bank deposits in your business Bank Account Check Register. To use this form, follow these instructions:

① On a daily or weekly basis, collect your Daily or Weekly Cash Reports. From each Report, record the following information:
+ Cash on hand at the beginning of the period
+ Cash taken in
+ Checks taken in
+ Cash paid out
+ The amount of the daily or weekly bank deposit
+ Cash on hand at the end of the period and after the bank deposit

② You can total the Deposit column as a cross-check against your Bank Account Check Register record of deposits.

DAILY CASH REPORT

Date:			Cash on Hand Beginning:					

	CASH OUT			CHECKS IN			CASH IN	
No.	Name	Amount		Name	Amount		Name	Amount
1								
2								
3								
4								
5								
6								
7								
8								
9								
10								
11								
12								
TOTAL								

Deposit No.:
Deposit Date:
Deposit Amount:
Deposited by:
Signed:

Total Cash In		
+ Total Checks In		
+ Cash on Hand Beginning		
= Total Receipts		
– Total Cash Out		
= Balance on Hand		
– Bank Deposit		
= Cash on Hand Ending		

WEEKLY CASH REPORT

Week of: Cash on Hand Beginning:

No.	CASH OUT			CHECKS IN			CASH IN		
	Name	Amount		Name	Amount		Name	Amount	
1									
2									
3									
4									
5									
6									
7									
8									
9									
10									
11									
12									
TOTAL									

Deposit No.:	
Deposit Date:	
Deposit Amount:	
Deposited by:	
Signed:	

Total Cash In		
+ Total Checks In		
+ Cash on Hand Beginning		
= Total Receipts		
– Total Cash Out		
= Balance on Hand		
– Bank Deposit		
= Cash on Hand Ending		

MONTHLY CASH REPORT SUMMARY

Date	On Hand		Cash In		Checks In		Cash Out		Deposit		On Hand	
1												
2												
3												
4												
5												
6												
7												
8												
9												
10												
11												
12												
13												
14												
15												
16												
17												
18												
19												
20												
21												
22												
23												
24												
25												
26												
27												
28												
29												
30												
31												

Tracking Income

The second feature of your business income tracking system should be a method to keep track of your actual income. This portion of the system will provide you with a list of all taxable and nontaxable income and of any sales taxes collected, if applicable. For sales tax information, please contact your state's sales tax revenue collection agency. If your state has a sales tax on the product or service that you provide, you will need accurate records to determine your total taxable and nontaxable income and the amount of sales tax that is due. For this purpose and for the purpose of tracking all of your income for your own business analysis, you should prepare a Daily or Weekly Income Record. The information from these reports then will be used to prepare Monthly and Annual Income Summaries.

Daily or Weekly Income Records

To use this form, do the following:

① Depending on the level of your business, decide which time period you would like to track on each form: daily or weekly. Fill in the appropriate date or time period.

② You will need to contact your state taxing agency for information on how to determine if a sale or the provision of a service is taxable or nontaxable. You also will need to determine the appropriate rates for sales tax collection.

③ For each item, record the following information:
   + Invoice number
   + Taxable income amount
   + Sales tax amount
   + Nontaxable income amount
   + Total income (Taxable, sales tax, nontaxable amounts combined)

④ On a daily or weekly basis, total the amounts in each column to determine the totals for the particular time period. These figures will be carried over to the Monthly and Annual Income Summaries that will be explained next.

Monthly Income Summary

① Fill in the appropriate month.

② Using your Daily or Weekly Income Records, record the following information for each day or week:
+ Total taxable income amount
+ Total sales tax amount
+ Total nontaxable income amount
+ Total income (taxable, sales tax, nontaxable amounts combined)

③ On a monthly basis, total the amounts in each column to determine the totals for the particular month. These figures will be carried over to the Annual Income Summary that will be explained next.

Annual Income Summary

① Fill in the year.

② On a monthly basis, carry the totals from all of the columns on your Monthly Income Summary form to the appropriate column of the Annual Income Summary form.

③ At the end of each quarter, total all of the monthly entries to arrive at your quarterly totals for each category.

④ To double-check your monthly calculations, total your categories across each month and put this total in the final column. Compare this total with the total on your Monthly Income Summary sheets. If there is a discrepancy, check each of your figures until you discover the error.

⑤ To double-check your quarterly calculations, total your monthly totals in the final quarterly column. This figure should equal the total of the quarterly category totals across the quarterly row. If there is a discrepancy, check each of your figures until you discover the error.

⑥ Finally, total each of your quarterly amounts to arrive at the annual totals. To cross check your calculations, total the quarterly totals in the final column. This figure should equal the total for all of the annual totals in each category across the Annual Total row. If there is a discrepancy, check each of your figures until you discover the error.

DAILY INCOME RECORD

Date of:

Invoice Number	Taxable Income		Sales Tax		Nontaxable Income		Total Income	
Daily TOTAL								

WEEKLY INCOME RECORD

Week of:

Invoice Number	Taxable Income		Sales Tax		Nontaxable Income		Total Income	
Weekly TOTAL								

MONTHLY INCOME SUMMARY

Month of:

Date	Taxable Income		Sales Tax		Nontaxable Income		Total Income	
1								
2								
3								
4								
5								
6								
7								
8								
9								
10								
11								
12								
13								
14								
15								
16								
17								
18								
19								
20								
21								
22								
23								
24								
25								
26								
27								
28								
29								
30								
31								
Monthly TOTAL								

ANNUAL INCOME SUMMARY

Year of:

Date	Taxable Income		Sales Tax		Nontaxable Income		Total Income	
January								
February								
March								
1st Quarter								
April								
May								
June								
2nd Quarter								
July								
August								
September								
3rd Quarter								
October								
November								
December								
4th Quarter								
Annual TOTAL								

Tracking Credit Sales

The final component of your business income tracking system will be a logical method to track your credit sales. You will use a Daily, Weekly, or Monthly Credit Sales Record to track the actual sales on credit, and a Credit Sales Aging Report to track the payment on these sales. In addition, several forms are provided for the billing of these credit sales: an Invoice, Statement, Past Due Statement, and Credit Memo.

Daily, Weekly, or Monthly Credit Sales Record

To keep track of sales made to customers on credit or on account, follow these directions:

① Depending on your particular level of business activity, decide whether you will need to use a Daily, Weekly, or Monthly Credit Sales Record.

② Fill in the appropriate date or time period.

③ For each sale that is made on credit, fill in the following information from the customer Invoice (see Invoice instructions later in this chapter):
  ✦ Invoice number
  ✦ Date of sale
  ✦ Customer name
  ✦ Total sale amount

④ The final column is for recording the date that the credit sale has been paid in full.

⑤ The information from your Daily, Weekly, or Monthly Credit Sales Record will also be used to prepare your Credit Sales Aging Report on a monthly basis.

DAILY CREDIT SALES RECORD

Month of:

Invoice No.	Sale Date	Customer	Sales Total		Date Paid

WEEKLY CREDIT SALES RECORD

Month of:

Invoice No.	Sale Date	Customer	Sales Total		Date Paid

MONTHLY CREDIT SALES RECORD

Month of:

Invoice No.	Sale Date	Customer	Sales Total		Date Paid

Credit Sales Aging Report

This report is used to track the current status of your credit sales or accounts receivables. Through the use of this form you will be able to track whether or not the people or companies that owe you money are falling behind on their payments. With this information, you will be able to determine how to handle these accounts: sending past due notices, halting sales to them, turning them over to a collection agency, etc. To use this form, do the following:

① Decide on which day of the month you would like to perform your credit sales aging calculations. Enter this date on the first line of the form.

② For each credit sales account, enter the name of the account from your Daily, Weekly, or Monthly Credit Sales Records.

③ In the Total column, enter the total current amount that is owed to you. If this figure is based on credit sales during the current month, enter this figure again in the Current column. Do this for each credit account.

④ Each month you will prepare a new Credit Sales Aging Report on a new sheet. On the same date in the next month, determine how much of the originally owed balance has been paid off. Enter the amount of the unpaid balance from the previous month in the 30–60 days column. Enter any new credit sales for the month under the Current column. The figure in the Total column should be the total of all of the columns to the right of the Total column.

⑤ Each month, determine how much was paid on the account, deduct that amount from the oldest amount due, and shift the amounts due over one column to the right. Add any new credit sales to the Current column and put the total of the amounts in the Total column.

⑥ After entering the information for each month, total each of the columns across the Total line at the bottom of the report. The Total column is 100 percent of the amount due. Calculate the percentage for each of the other columns to determine how much of your accounts receivable are 30, 60, 90, or more than 90 days overdue.

CREDIT SALES AGING REPORT

Account Name	Total		Current		30-60 Days		60-90 Days		90+ Days	
TOTAL										
PERCENT	100%									

Invoices and Statements

For credit sales, you will need to provide each customer with a current Invoice. You also will need to send them a Statement if the balance is not paid within the first 30 days. In addition, you will need to send a Past Due Statement if the balance becomes overdue. Finally, a form is provided to record instances when a customer is given credit for a returned item. You will need to produce two copies of each of these forms: one for your records and one for the customer.

Invoice

The invoice is your key credit sales document. To prepare and track invoices, follow these directions:

① Make a number of copies of the invoice form. You can insert your business card in the upper left corner before copying. Number each form consecutively. Make a copy of the form when the form is sent out to the customer using either carbon paper or a copy machine.

② For each order, fill in the following information:
- Date
- The name and address of who will be billed for the order
- The name and address where the order will be shipped
- The item number of the product or service sold
- The quantity ordered
- The description of the item
- The per unit price of the item
- The total amount billed (quantity times per unit price)

③ Subtotal all of the items where shown. Add any sales taxes and shipping costs and total the Balance.

④ Record the pertinent information from the Invoice on the appropriate Daily, Weekly, or Monthly Credit Sales Record.

⑤ Record the pertinent information from the Invoice on the appropriate Daily, Weekly, or Monthly Income Record.

⑥ Send one copy of the Invoice to the customer with the order and file the other copy in a file for your invoices.

INVOICE

Date
Invoice No.

Bill to:

Ship to:

Item No.	Quantity	Description	Price		Amount	
			Subtotal			
			Tax			
			Shipping			
			BALANCE			

Statement and Past Due Statement

Statements are used to send your credit customers a notice of the amount that is currently due. Statements are generally sent at 30-day intervals, beginning either 30 days after the invoice is sent, or at the beginning of the next month or the next cycle for sending statements. Follow these instructions for preparing your statements:

① You should decide on a statement billing cycle. Generally, this is a specific date each month (for example: the first, tenth, or fifteenth of each month).

② Make a copy of the Statement form using your business card in the upper left corner. Fill in the date and the account name and address.

③ In the body of the form, enter information from any Invoice that is still unpaid as of the date you are completing the Statement. You should enter the following items for each unpaid Invoice:
   + The date of the Invoice
   + A description (including Invoice number) of the Invoice
   + Any payments received since the last statement or since the sale
   + The amount still owed on that Invoice

④ When all of the invoice information for all of the customer's invoices has been entered, total the Amounts column and enter at Balance. The information on the Statement then can be used to enter information on your Credit Sales Aging Report.

⑤ The Past Due Statement is simply a version of the basic Statement that includes a notice that the account is past due. This Past Due Statement should be sent when the account becomes overdue. Fill it out in the same manner used for Statements.

STATEMENT

Date

Account:

Date	Description	Payment		Amount	
	Please pay this BALANCE				

PAST DUE STATEMENT

Date

Account:

This Account is now Past Due. Please pay upon receipt to avoid collection costs.

Date	Description	Payment		Amount	

Please pay this BALANCE

Credit Memo

The final form for tracking your business income is the Credit Memo. This form is used to provide you and your customer with a written record of any credit given for goods that have been returned by the customer. You will need to set a policy regarding when such credit will be given, (for example: whether only for a certain time period after the sale, or for defects, or other limitations). To use the Credit Memo, follow these instructions:

1. Make copies of the Credit Memo using your business card in the upper left corner. You will need to make two copies of the Credit Memo when filled in: one for your records and one for your customer to keep.

2. Fill in the date, the number of the original Invoice, and the customer's name and address.

3. Fill in the following information in the body of the Credit Memo:
   + Item number of item returned
   + Quantity of items returned
   + Description of item returned
   + Unit price of item returned
   + Total amount of credit (quantity times unit price)

4. Subtotal the credit for all items. Add any appropriate sales tax credit and total the amount in the Credit box. This is the amount that will be credited or refunded to the customer.

5. In the lower left box, indicate the reason for the return, any necessary approval, and the date of the approval.

6. Handle the Credit Memo like a negative Invoice. Record the amount of credit as a negative on the appropriate Daily or Weekly Income Record.

7. Record the pertinent information from the Credit Memo as a negative amount on the appropriate Daily, Weekly, or Monthly Credit Sales Record, if the Credit Memo applies to a previous sale on credit that was recorded on a Credit Sales Record.

131

CREDIT MEMO

Date
Order No.
Credit to:

GOODS RETURNED

Item No.	Quantity	Description	Price		Amount	

Reason for return:		Subtotal	
Approved by:		Tax	
Date:		CREDIT	

Payroll

One of the most difficult and complex accounting functions that small businesses face is their payroll. Because of the various state and Federal taxes that must be applied and because of the myriad government forms that must be prepared, the handling of a business payroll often causes accounting nightmares. Even if there is only one employee, there is a potential for problems.

First, let's examine the basics. If your business is a sole proprietorship and you are the only one who works in the business, there is no need for a formal payroll system. You may pay for yourself on a periodic schedule, but these payments are not considered deductions for the business. They are simply draws and no taxes are withheld. You will need to file and pay estimated taxes as an individual on the amount of money that you expect your business to net each year. These payments are made quarterly and are handled on IRS Form 1040-ES: *Estimated Tax for Individuals*. You also will be required to pay a self-employment tax to the federal government. This is equivalent to a payroll deduction for Social Security and Medicare taxes. This is handled with IRS Schedule SE: *Self-Employment Tax* and is filed with your annual personal income taxes.

If you operate as a partnership and there are no employees, the same rules apply. The partnership net income will be passed through to you as a partner and you will be liable for individual income taxes on your share. Any draws which you take against the partnership will not be considered business deductions for the business. If your business is a corporation, all pay must be handled as payroll, even if you are the only employee. The corporation is a separate entity and the corporation itself will be the employer. You and any other people which you hire will be the employees. Follow the instructions for business payroll explained later in this chapter.

If you operate as a sole proprietorship or partnership and you have employees, you must also follow the entire business payroll details that are explained in this chapter. Business payroll entails a great deal of paperwork and has numerous government tax filing deadlines. You will be required to make payroll tax deposits, file various quarterly payroll tax returns, and make additional end-of-the-year reports.

Initially, if you have any employees, you must take certain steps to set up your payroll and official status as an employer. The following information contains only the instructions for meeting federal requirements. Please check with your particular state and local governments for information regarding any additional payroll tax, state unemployment insurance, or worker's compensation requirements. The requirements below will apply to any business which decides to be come an employer, whether it is a sole proprietorship, partnership, or S- or C-corporation.

Setting Up Your Payroll

① The first step in becoming an employer is to file IRS Form SS-4: *Application for Employer Identification Number* (FEIN). This will officially register your business with the Federal government as an employer. This form and instructions are included on the Forms-on-CD.

② Next, each employee must fill in an IRS Form W-4: *Employee's Withholding Allowance Certificate*. This will provide you with the necessary information regarding withholding allowances to enable you to prepare your payroll.

③ You must then determine the gross salary or wage that each employee will earn. For each employee, complete an Employee Payroll Record and prepare a Quarterly Payroll Time Sheet as explained later in this chapter.

④ You will then need to consult the tables in IRS Circular E: *Employer's Tax Guide*. From the tables in this publication, you will be able to determine the proper deductions for each employee for each pay period. If your employees are paid on an hourly basis and the number of hours worked is different each pay period, you will have to perform these calculations for each pay period.

⑤ Before you pay your employee, you should open a separate business bank account for handling your business payroll tax deductions and payments. This will allow you to immediately deposit all taxes due into this separate account and help prevent the lack of sufficient money available when the taxes are due.

⑥ Next you will pay your employee and record the deduction information on the Employee's Payroll Record.

⑦ When you have completed paying all of your employees for the pay period, you will write a separate check for the total amount of all of your employees' deductions and for the total amount of any employer's share of taxes. You will then deposit this check into your business payroll tax bank account that you set up in item number five above.

⑧ At the end of every month, you will need to transfer the information regarding employee deductions to your Payroll Depository Record and Annual Payroll Summary. Copies of these forms are included later in this chapter. You will then also calculate your employer share of Social Security and Medicare taxes. Each month (or quarter if your tax liability is less than $500.00 per quarter), you will need to deposit the correct amount of taxes due with the Federal government. This is done either by making a monthly payment for the taxes due to your bank with IRS Form 8109: *Tax Deposit Coupon* or by making the payment on a quarterly basis when you file IRS Form 941: *Employer's Quarterly Federal Tax Return.*

(9) On a quarterly or annual basis, you also will need to make a tax payment for Federal Unemployment Tax, using IRS Form 940 or IRS Form 940-EZ: *Employer's Annual Federal Unemployment Tax Return* (FUTA). This tax is solely the responsibility of the employer and is not deducted from the employee's pay. Also on a quarterly basis, you will need to file IRS Form 941: *Employer's Quarterly Federal Tax Return.* If you have made monthly deposits of your taxes due, there will be no quarterly taxes to pay, but you still will need to file these forms quarterly.

(10) Finally, to complete your payroll, at the end of the year you must do the following:
   ✦ Prepare IRS Form W-2: *Wage and Tax Statement* for each employee
   ✦ File IRS Form W-3: *Transmittal of Wage and Tax Statements*

Remember that your state and local tax authorities generally will have additional requirements and taxes that will need to be paid. In many jurisdictions, these requirements are tailored after the Federal requirements and the procedures and due dates are similar.

Quarterly Payroll Time Sheet

On the following page is a Quarterly Payroll Time Sheet. If your employees are paid an hourly wage, you will prepare a sheet like this for each employee for each quarter during the year. On this sheet you will keep track of the following information:

- Number of hours worked (daily, weekly, and quarterly)
- Number of regular and overtime hours worked

The information from this Quarterly Payroll Time Sheet will be transferred to your individual Employee Payroll Record in order to calculate the employee's paycheck amounts. This is explained following the Quarterly Payroll Time Sheet.

QUARTERLY PAYROLL TIME SHEET

Employee:

Week of	Sun	Mon	Tue	Wed	Thu	Fri	Sat	Reg	OT	Total
Quarterly TOTAL										

Employee Payroll Record

You will use this form to track each employee's payroll information.

① For each employee, fill in the following information at the top of the form:
   + Name and address of employee
   + Employee's Social Security number
   + Number of exemptions claimed by employee on Form W-4
   + Regular and overtime wage rates
   + Pay period (ie., weekly, biweekly, monthly, etc.)

② For each pay period, fill in the number of regular and overtime hours worked from the employee's Quarterly Payroll Time Sheet. Multiply this amount by the employee's wage rate to determine the gross pay. For example: 40 hours at the regular wage of $8.00/hour = $320.00; plus five hours at the overtime wage rate of $12.00/hour = $60.00. Gross pay for the period is $320.00 + $60.00 = $380.00.

③ Determine the federal withholding tax deduction for the pay amount by consulting the withholding tax tables in IRS Circular E: *Employer's Tax Guide*. Enter this figure on the form. For example: In 2001 for a single person with no dependents, claiming only one exemption, and paid weekly, the withholding tax for $380.00 would be $42.00.

④ Determine the employee's share of Social Security and Medicare deductions. As of 2001, the employee's Social Security share rate is 12.4 percent and the employee's Medicare share rate is 2.9 percent. Multiply these rates times the employee's gross wages and enter the figures in the appropriate places. For example: for $380.00, the Social Security deduction would be $380.00 x .124 = $47.12 and the Medicare deduction would be $380.00 x .029 = $11.02.

⑤ Determine any state or local taxes and enter in the appropriate column.

⑥ Subtract all of the deductions from the employee's gross wages to determine the employee's net pay. Enter this figure in the final column and prepare the employee's paycheck using the deduction information from this sheet. Also prepare a check to your payroll tax bank account for a total of the federal withholding amount and two times the Social Security and Medicare amounts. This includes your employer share of these taxes. The employer's share of Social Security and Medicare taxes is equal to the employee's share.

EMPLOYEE PAYROLL RECORD

Employee Name: Social Security Number:

Address: Number of Exemptions:

                                        Rate of Pay: Overtime:

                                        Pay Period:

Date	Check #	Period	Hours	OT	Gross	Fed	SS	Med	State	Net
Period TOTAL										

Payroll Depository Record

You will be required to deposit taxes with the IRS on a monthly or quarterly basis (unless your total employment taxes totaled more than $50,000.00 for the previous year, in which case you should obviously consult an accountant). If your employment taxes total less than $500.00 per quarter, you may pay your payroll tax liability when you quarterly file your Federal Form 941: *Employer's Quarterly Federal Tax Return*. If your payroll tax liability is more than $500.00 per quarter, you must deposit your payroll taxes on a monthly basis with a bank using IRS Form 8109: *Federal Tax Deposit Coupon*. To track your payroll tax liability, use the Payroll Depository Record following these instructions:

① On a monthly basis, total each column on all of your Employee Payroll Records. This will give you a figure for each employee's federal withholding tax, Social Security tax, and Medicare tax for the month.

② Total all of the federal withholding taxes for all employees for the month and enter this figure in the appropriate column on the Payroll Depository Record.

③ Total Social Security and Medicare taxes for all of your employees for the entire month and enter this figure in the appropriate columns on the Payroll Depository Record. Note that SS/EE refers to Social Security/Employee's Share and that MC/EE refers to Medicare/Employee's Share.

④ Enter identical amounts in the SS/ER and MC/ER columns as you have entered in the SS/EE and MC/EE columns. The employer's share of Social Security and Medicare is the same as the employee's share, but is not deducted from the employee's pay.

⑤ Total all of the deductions for the month. This is the amount of your total monthly federal payroll tax liability. If necessary, write a check to your local bank for this amount and deposit it using IRS Form 8109: *Federal Tax Deposit Coupon*.

⑥ If you must file only quarterly, total all three of your monthly amounts on a quarterly basis and pay this amount when you file your IRS Form 941: *Employer's Quarterly Federal Tax Return*. On a yearly basis, total all of the quarterly columns to arrive at your total annual federal payroll tax liability.

PAYROLL DEPOSITORY RECORD

Month	Fed W/H	SS/EE	SS/ER	MC/EE	MC/ER	Total
January						
February						
March						
1st Quarter						
1st Quarter Total Number of Employees:			Total Wages Paid:			
April						
May						
June						
2nd Quarter						
2nd Quarter Total Number of Employees:			Total Wages Paid:			
July						
August						
September						
3rd Quarter						
3rd Quarter Total Number of Employees:			Total Wages Paid:			
October						
November						
December						
4th Quarter						
4th Quarter Total Number of Employees:			Total Wages Paid:			
Yearly TOTAL						
Yearly Total Number of Employees:			Total Wages Paid:			

Annual Payroll Summary

The final payroll form is used to total all of the payroll amounts for all employees on a monthly, quarterly, and annual basis. Much of the information on this form is similar to the information that you compiled for the Payroll Depository Record. However, the purpose of this form is to provide you with a record of all of your payroll costs, including the payroll deduction costs. This form will be useful for both tax and planning purposes as you examine your business profitability on a quarterly and annual basis. Follow these directions to prepare this form:

① For each month, transfer the amounts for federal withholding from the Payroll Depository Record to this form.

② For each month, total the columns on your Payroll Depository form for SS/EE and SS/ER and also for MC/EE and MC/ER. You will then simply need to transfer the totals for Social Security and Medicare taxes to this form. Recall that SS refers to Social Security, MC refers to Medicare, EE refers to Employee, and ER refers to Employer.

③ For each month, total all of your employees' gross and net pay amounts from their individual Employee Payroll Records and transfer these totals to this form.

④ On a quarterly basis, total the columns to determine your quarterly payroll costs. Annually, total the quarterly amounts to determine your annual costs.

ANNUAL PAYROLL SUMMARY

	Gross		Fed		SS		MC		State		Net	
January												
February												
March												
1st Quarter Total												
April												
May												
June												
2nd Quarter Total												
July												
August												
September												
3rd Quarter Total												
October												
November												
December												
4th Quarter Total												
Yearly TOTAL												

Profit and Loss Statements

A Profit and Loss Statement is the key financial statement for presenting how your business is performing over a period of time. The Profit and Loss Statement illuminates both the amounts of money that your business has spent on expenses and the amounts of money that your business has taken in over a specific period of time. You may choose to prepare a profit and loss statement monthly, quarterly, or annually, depending on your particular needs. At a minimum, you will need to have an annual profit and loss statement in order to streamline your tax return preparation.

A Profit and Loss Statement, however, provides much more than assistance in easing your tax preparation burdens. It allows you to clearly view the performance of your business over a particular time period. As you begin to collect a series of profit and loss statements, you will be able to conduct various analyses of your business. For example, you will be able to compare monthly performances over a single year to determine which month was the best or worst for your business. Quarterly results will also be able to be contrasted. The comparison of several annual expense and revenue figures will allow you to judge the growth or shrinkage of your business over time. Numerous other comparisons are possible, depending on your particular business. How have sales been influenced by advertising expenses? Are production costs higher this quarter than last? Do seasons have an impact on sales? Are certain expenses becoming a burden on the business? The profit and loss statement is one of the key financial statements for the analysis of your business. Along with the balance sheet, the profit and loss statement should become an integral part of both your short- and long-range business planning.

This section will explain how to compile the information that you will need to prepare your profit and loss statements. All of the necessary information to prepare your profit and loss statement will be obtained from the financial records which you have prepared using this book. No other sources will be necessary to complete your profit and loss statements.

Profit and Loss Statements

You may use this Profit and Loss Statement to obtain a clearer picture of your business performance. At a minimum, each year at year's end you will need to prepare the Annual Profit and Loss Statement to assist you in tax preparation. If you desire, you may prepare a Monthly or Quarterly version of this form to help with your business planning. To prepare this form:

① Choose either the Monthly, Quarterly, or Annual Profit and Loss Statement. The first figure you will need will be your Gross Sales Income. This figure will come from your monthly, quarterly, or annual Total Sales figures on your Annual Income

Summary sheet. If your business is a pure service business, put your income on the Service Income Total line. If your business income comes from part sales and part service, place the appropriate figures on the correct lines.

② Next, if your business sells items from inventory, you will need to calculate your monthly, quarterly, or annual Cost of Goods Sold. Monthly or quarterly, you may need to do a quick inventory count in order to have the necessary figures to make this computation. Annually, you will need to perform a thorough inventory. Fill in the Cost of Goods Sold figure on the Profit and Loss Statement. If your business is a pure service business, skip this line. Determine your Net Sales Income by subtracting your Cost of Goods Sold from your Gross Sales Income.

③ Calculate your Total Income for the period by adding your Net Sales Income and your Total Service Income and any Miscellaneous Income (for example, interest earned on a checking account).

④ To obtain your Expenses figure, consult your Annual Expense Summary sheet. Fill in the appropriate Expense Account categories on the Profit and Loss Statement. If you have a large number of categories, you may need to prepare a second sheet. Transfer either the monthly, quarterly, or annual totals for each of your separate expense accounts to the Profit and Loss Statement. Add in any Miscellaneous Expenses.

⑤ Total all of your expenses and subtract your Total Expense figure from your Total Income figure to determine your Pre-Tax Profit for the time period.

MONTHLY PROFIT AND LOSS STATEMENT

For the month of:

	INCOME		
Income	Gross Sales Income		
	Less Cost of Goods Sold		
	Net Sales Income Total		
	Service Income Total		
	Miscellaneous Income Total		
	Total Income		

	EXPENSES		
Expenses	Account Number		
	Account Number		
	Account Number		
	Account Number		
	Account Number		
	Account Number		
	Account Number		
	Account Number		
	Account Number		
	Account Number		
	Account Number		
	Account Number		
	General Expenses Total		
	Miscellaneous Expenses		
	Total Expenses		

Pre-Tax Profit (Income less Expenses)	

QUARTERLY PROFIT AND LOSS STATEMENT

For the quarter of:

	INCOME		
Income	Gross Sales Income		
	Less Cost of Goods Sold		
	Net Sales Income Total		
	Service Income Total		
	Miscellaneous Income Total		
	Total Income		

	EXPENSES		
Expenses	Account Number		
	Account Number		
	Account Number		
	Account Number		
	Account Number		
	Account Number		
	Account Number		
	Account Number		
	Account Number		
	Account Number		
	Account Number		
	Account Number		
	General Expenses Total		
	Miscellaneous Expenses		
	Total Expenses		

Pre-Tax Profit (Income less Expenses)	

ANNUAL PROFIT AND LOSS STATEMENT

For the year of:

INCOME			
Income	Gross Sales Income		
	Less Cost of Goods Sold		
	Net Sales Income Total		
	Service Income Total		
	Miscellaneous Income Total		
	Total Income		

EXPENSES			
Expenses	Account Number		
	Account Number		
	Account Number		
	Account Number		
	Account Number		
	Account Number		
	Account Number		
	Account Number		
	Account Number		
	Account Number		
	Account Number		
	Account Number		
	General Expenses Total		
	Miscellaneous Expenses		
	Total Expenses		

Pre-Tax Profit (Income less Expenses)	

Balance Sheets

A profit and loss statement provides a view of business operations over a particular period of time. It allows a look at the income and expenses and profit or losses of the business during the time period. In contrast, a Balance Sheet is designed to be a look at the financial position of a company on a specific date. It shows what the business owns and owes on a fixed date. Its purpose is to depict the financial strength of a company as shown by its assets and liabilities. Recall that the assets minus liabilities equals equity (or net worth). Essentially, the Balance Sheet shows what the company would be worth if all of the assets were sold and all of the liabilities were paid off. A value is placed on each asset and each liability. These figures are then balanced by adjusting the value of the owner's equity figure in the equation. Your Balance Sheet will total your current and fixed assets and your current and long-term liabilities. You may choose to prepare a Balance Sheet monthly, quarterly, or annually. At a minimum, you will need to prepare a Balance Sheet at year's end. For corporations and partnerships, this is a requirement. For sole proprietorships, this is highly recommended.

① Your Current Assets consist of the following items. Where to obtain the correct figure for the asset amount is shown after each item:
  + Cash in Bank (from your Check Register Balance)
  + Cash on Hand (from your Petty Cash Register and your Monthly Cash Report)
  + Accounts Receivable (from your Credit Sales Aging Reports)
  + Inventory (from a Physical Inventory Report annually or from a review of your Perpetual or Periodic Inventory monthly or quarterly)
  + Prepaid Expense (These may be rent, insurance, or similar items which have been paid for prior to their actual use. Check through your Monthly Expense Summary to determine which items may be considered prepaid expenses)

② Total all of your Current Assets on your Balance Sheet.

③ Your Fixed Assets consist of the following items. Where to obtain the correct figure for the asset amount is shown after each item:
  + Equipment (from your Fixed Asset Account sheets. You will need to update these sheets to include any equipment purchased since your last update. Update from your Monthly Expense Record sheets)
  + Autos and Trucks (from your Fixed Asset Account sheets. You will need to update these sheets to include any vehicles purchased since your last update. Update from your Monthly Expense Record sheets)
  + Buildings (from your Fixed Asset Account sheets. You will need to update these sheets to include any buildings purchased since your last update. Update from your Monthly Expense Record sheets)

④ Total your Fixed Assets (except land) on your Balance Sheet. Now, returning to your Fixed Asset sheets, total all of the depreciation which you have previously deducted for all of your fixed assets (except land). Include in this figure any business deductions which you have taken for Section 179 write-offs of business equipment. Enter this total depreciation figure under Depreciation and subtract this figure from the total Fixed Assets (except land) figure.

⑤ Now, enter the value for any land which your business owns. Recall that land may not be depreciated. Add Fixed Asset amount less Depreciation and the value of the land. This is your total Fixed Asset value.

⑥ Add any Miscellaneous Assets not yet included. These may consist of stocks, bonds, or other business investments. Total your Current, Fixed, and Miscellaneous Assets to arrive at your total Assets figure.

⑦ Your Current Liabilities consist of the following items. Where to obtain the correct figure for the liability amount is shown after each item:
- Accounts Payable (from your Accounts Payable Record sheets)
- Taxes Payable (from two sources: your sales taxes payable figure comes from your Monthly Income Summary sheets and your payroll taxes payable from the Check Register of your special payroll tax bank account. Include any amounts which have been collected but not yet paid to the state or federal government
- Miscellaneous Current Liabilities (include here the principal due on any short-term notes payable. Also include any interest on credit purchases, notes, or loans which has accrued but not been paid, the current amounts due on any long-term liabilities, and any payroll which has accrued but not yet been paid)

⑧ Your Long-Term Liabilities consist of the principal of any long-term note, loan, or mortgage due. Any current amounts due should be listed as a Current Liability.

⑨ Total your Current and Long-Term Liabilities to arrive at a Total Liabilities Figure.

⑩ Subtract your Total Liabilities from your Total Assets to arrive at your Owner's Equity. For a sole proprietor, this figure represents the Net Worth of your business. For a partnership, this figure represents the value of the partner's original investments plus any earnings and less any partner draws. For a corporation, this figure represents the total of contributions by the owners or stockholders plus earnings after paying any dividends. Total liabilities and owner's equity will always equal Total Assets.

CURRENT BALANCE SHEET

As of:

ASSETS			
Current Assets	Cash in Bank		
	Cash on Hand		
	Accounts Receivable		
	Inventory		
	Prepaid Expenses		
	Total Current Assets		
Fixed Assets	Equipment (cost)		
	Autos and Trucks (cost)		
	Buildings (cost)		
	Total		
	(Less Depreciation)		
	Net Total		
	Add Land (cost)		
	Total Fixed Assets		
	Total Miscellaneous Assets		
	Total Assets		

LIABILITIES			
Current Liabilities	Accounts Payable		
	Taxes Payable		
	Total Current Liabilities		
Fixed Liabilities	Loans Payable (long-term)		
	Total Fixed Liabilities		
	Total Liabilities		
Owner's Equity	Net Worth or Capital Surplus + Stock Value		

MONTHLY BALANCE SHEET

As of:

ASSETS			
Current Assets	Cash in Bank		
	Cash on Hand		
	Accounts Receivable		
	Inventory		
	Prepaid Expenses		
	Total Current Assets		
Fixed Assets	Equipment (cost)		
	Autos and Trucks (cost)		
	Buildings (cost)		
	Total		
	(Less Depreciation)		
	Net Total		
	Add Land (cost)		
	Total Fixed Assets		
	Total Miscellaneous Assets		
	Total Assets		

LIABILITIES			
Current Liabilities	Accounts Payable		
	Taxes Payable		
	Total Current Liabilities		
Fixed Liabilities	Loans Payable (long-term)		
	Total Fixed Liabilities		
	Total Liabilities		
Owner's Equity	Net Worth or Capital Surplus + Stock Value		

QUARTERLY BALANCE SHEET

As of:

ASSETS			
Current Assets	Cash in Bank		
	Cash on Hand		
	Accounts Receivable		
	Inventory		
	Prepaid Expenses		
	Total Current Assets		
Fixed Assets	Equipment (cost)		
	Autos and Trucks (cost)		
	Buildings (cost)		
	Total		
	(Less Depreciation)		
	Net Total		
	Add Land (cost)		
	Total Fixed Assets		
	Total Miscellaneous Assets		
	Total Assets		

LIABILITIES			
Current Liabilities	Accounts Payable		
	Taxes Payable		
	Total Current Liabilities		
Fixed Liabilities	Loans Payable (long-term)		
	Total Fixed Liabilities		
	Total Liabilities		
Owner's Equity	Net Worth or Capital Surplus + Stock Value		

ANNUAL BALANCE SHEET

As of:

ASSETS			
Current Assets	Cash in Bank		
	Cash on Hand		
	Accounts Receivable		
	Inventory		
	Prepaid Expenses		
	Total Current Assets		
Fixed Assets	Equipment (cost)		
	Autos and Trucks (cost)		
	Buildings (cost)		
	Total		
	(Less Depreciation)		
	Net Total		
	Add Land (cost)		
	Total Fixed Assets		
	Total Miscellaneous Assets		
	Total Assets		
LIABILITIES			
Current Liabilities	Accounts Payable		
	Taxes Payable		
	Total Current Liabilities		
Fixed Liabilities	Loans Payable (long-term)		
	Total Fixed Liabilities		
	Total Liabilities		
Owner's Equity	Net Worth or Capital Surplus + Stock Value		

Chapter 3

Federal Income Tax Forms Checklists and Schedules

Taxation of C-Corporations

Corporations are a separate entity under the law and as such are subject to taxation at both the state and Federal levels. In general, C-corporations are subject to Federal income tax on the annual profits in many ways similar to the tax on individual income. However, there are significant differences. The most important aspect is the "double" taxation on corporate income if it is distributed to the shareholders in the form of dividends. At the corporate level, corporate net income is subject to tax at the corporate level. Corporate funds that are distributed to officers or directors in the forms of salaries, expense reimbursements, or employee benefits may be used by a corporation as a legitimate business deduction against the income of the corporation. Corporate surplus funds that are paid out to shareholders in the form of dividends on their ownership of stock in the corporation, however, are not allowed to be used as a corporate deduction. Thus, any funds used in this manner have been subject to corporate income tax prior to distribution to the shareholders. The dividends then are also subject to taxation as income to the individual shareholder and so are subject to a "double" taxation. S-corporations are taxed similarly to partnerships, with the corporation acting only as a conduit and all of the deductions and income passing to the individual shareholders, where they are subject to income tax. Corporations, however, may be used by businesses in many ways to actually lessen the Federal and state income tax burdens. A competent tax professional should be consulted. A chart of tax forms is provided, which details which IRS forms may be necessary. In addition, monthly, quarterly, and annual schedules of tax filings are also provided. A study of these tax forms and schedules will provide a brief overview of the method by which corporations are taxed. A basic comprehension of the information required on Federal tax forms will help you understand why certain financial records are necessary and will assist you as you decide how to organize your business financial records.

Taxation of Limited Liability Companies

There may be certain tax advantages to the operation of a business as a limited liability company. There are three methods by which a limited liability company may be taxed at the Federal level. The choice of method is, for the most part, up to the member(s) of the company. The checklists provided in this chapter are separated into these three general divisions.

Taxation As a Partnership

All limited liability companies that have more than one member will be taxed at the Federal level as a partnership, unless the members elect otherwise. The partnership taxation is automatic and does not require any election or filing of any form for the election. If, however, a limited liability company elects to be taxed as a regular corporation, the members must vote to make this election and they must file IRS Form 8832: *Entity Classification Election*. If corporate taxation is elected, see below under "Taxation As a Corporation."

If the limited liability company is to be taxed as a partnership, the profits generated by the limited liability company may be distributed directly to the members without incurring any "double" tax liability, as is the case with the distribution of corporate profits in the form of dividends to the shareholders. Income from a limited liability company is taxed at the personal income tax rate of each individual member. Note, however, that depending on the individual tax situation of each member, this aspect could prove to be a disadvantage. The losses of a limited liability company are also distributed directly to each member at the end of each fiscal year and may be written off as deductions by each individual member. Tax credits also are handled in a similar fashion. A list of necessary tax forms for limited liability companies being taxed as partnerships is included at the end of this chapter.

Taxation As a Corporation

All limited liability companies, whether they have only one member or many, may elect to be taxed at the Federal level as a corporation. This corporate taxation is not automatic and requires the filing of IRS Form 8832: *Entity Classification Election*. The company should complete this form, checking the box stating "Initial classification by a newly-formed entity (or change in current classification of an existing entity to take effect on January 1, 1997)." Under "Form of Entity" on this form, the limited liability

155

company should check the box in front of the statement: "A domestic eligible entity electing to be classified as an association taxable as a corporation." This will cause the limited liability company to be taxed as a corporation.

If the limited liability company is to be taxed as a corporation, the profits generated by the limited liability company will not pass through directly to the member, as with taxation of sole proprietorships or partnerships. Indeed, taxation of corporations opens the company up to "double" tax liability, in that any corporate profits are first taxed at the corporate level, and then the distribution of corporate profits in the form of dividends to the shareholders (or members) is taxed at the individual level at the personal income tax rates of the members. Note, however, that depending on the individual tax situation of the member, this aspect could prove to be an advantage. For a limited liability company that elects to be taxed as a corporation, the business losses are also not distributed directly to the member as individual deductions, but rather serve as deductions only for the company against company income. Tax credits are also handled in a similar fashion. A list of necessary tax forms for limited liability companies being taxed as corporations is included at the end of this chapter.

Taxation As a Sole Proprietorship

All limited liability companies that have only one member will be taxed at the Federal level as a sole proprietorship, unless the sole member elects otherwise. The sole proprietorship taxation requires the filing of IRS Form 8832: *Entity Classification Election*. The single-member company should complete this form, checking the box stating "Initial classification by a newly-formed entity (or change in current classification of an existing entity to take effect on January 1, 1997)." Under "Form of Entity" on this form, the single-member limited liability company should check the box in front of the statement: "A domestic eligible entity with a single owner electing to be disregarded as a separate entity." This will cause the single-member limited liability company to be taxed as a sole proprietorship. If, however, a single-member limited liability company elects to be taxed as a regular corporation, the member must also file IRS Form 8832: *Entity Classification Election*. If corporate taxation is elected, see above under "Taxation As a Corporation."

If the limited liability company is to be taxed as a sole proprietorship, the profits generated by the limited liability company pass through directly to the sole member without incurring any "double" tax liability, as is the case with the distribution of corporate profits in the form of dividends to the shareholders. Income from a limited liability company is taxed at the personal income tax rate of the sole member. Note, however, that depending on the individual tax situation of the member, this aspect could prove to be a disadvantage. The losses of a limited liability company are also distributed directly to the member as individual deductions. Tax credits are also handled in a similar fashion. A list of necessary tax forms for limited liability companies being taxed as sole proprietorships is included at the end of this chapter.

For a detailed understanding of the individual tax consequences of operating your business as a limited liability company, a competent tax professional should be consulted. The financial records that you will compile using the forms in this book and Forms-on-CD will make your tax preparation much easier, whether you handle this yourself or it is handled by a tax professional. A basic comprehension of the information required on Federal tax forms will help you understand why certain financial records are necessary. Understanding tax reporting will also assist you as you decide how to organize your business financial records.

Various checklists of tax forms are provided that detail which IRS forms may be necessary for each method of taxation of limited liability companies. In addition, you may wish to review the tax filing schedules for the entity classification you choose for your company.

Taxation of Partnerships

There may be certain tax advantages to operation of a business as a partnership. The profits generated by a partnership may be distributed directly to the partners without incurring any "double" tax liability, as is the case with the distribution of corporate profits in the form of dividends to the shareholders. Income from a partnership is taxed at personal income tax rates. Note, however, that depending on the individual tax situation of each partner, this aspect could prove to be a disadvantage. The losses of a partnership are also distributed directly to each partner at the end of each fiscal year and may be written off as deductions by each individual partner. Tax credits are also handled in a similar fashion.

For a detailed understanding about the individual tax consequences of operating your business as a partnership, a competent tax professional should be consulted. The financial records that you will compile using the forms in this book will make your tax preparation much easier, whether you handle this yourself or it is handled by a tax professional. A basic comprehension of the information required on Federal tax forms will help you understand why certain financial records are necessary. Understanding tax reporting will also assist you as you decide how to organize your business financial records.

A chart of tax forms is provided that details which IRS forms may be necessary. In addition, a schedule of tax filing is also provided to assist you in keeping your tax reporting timely.

Taxation of S-Corporations

Corporations are a separate entity under the law and as such are subject to taxation at both the state and Federal levels. As noted earlier, there are two types of corporations: C-corporations and S-corporations. The difference between the two is in the area of taxation. In general, C-corporations are subject to Federal income tax on the annual profits in many ways similar to the tax on individual income. However, there are significant differences. The most important aspect is the "double" taxation on corporate income if it is distributed to the shareholders in the form of dividends. At the corporate level, corporate net income is subject to tax at the corporate level. Corporate funds that are distributed to officers or directors in the form of salaries, expense reimbursements, or employee benefits may be used by a corporation as a legitimate business deduction against the income of the corporation. Corporate surplus funds that are paid out to shareholders in the form of dividends on their ownership of stock in the corporation, however, are not allowed to be used as a corporate deduction. Thus, any funds used in this manner have been subject to corporate income tax prior to distribution to the shareholders. The dividends are then also subject to taxation as income to the individual shareholder and so are subject to a "double" taxation.

S-corporations are taxed similarly to partnerships, with the corporation acting only as a conduit and all of the deductions and income passing to the individual shareholders where they are subject to income tax. The S-corporation does not pay a corporate tax and files a different type of tax return than does a standard corporation. Taxation of the profits of the S-corporation falls to the individuals who own shares in the corporation. This also allows for each individual shareholder to personally deduct their share of any corporate losses. Corporations in general, however, may be used by businesses in many ways to actually lessen the Federal and state income tax burdens. A competent tax professional should be consulted. The financial records that you will compile using the forms in this book will make your tax preparation much easier, whether you handle this yourself or it is handled by a tax professional. A basic comprehension of the information required on Federal tax forms will help you understand why certain financial records are necessary. Understanding tax reporting will also assist you as you decide how to organize your business financial records.

A chart of tax forms is provided detailing which IRS forms may be necessary. In addition, a schedule of tax filing is also provided to assist you in keeping your tax reporting timely.

Taxation of Sole Proprietorships

The taxation of sole proprietorships is a relatively easy concept to understand. The sole proprietorship is not considered a separate entity for Federal tax purposes. Thus, all of the profits and losses of the business are simply personal and individual profits or losses of the sole owner. They are reported on IRS Schedule C: *Profits or Losses of a Business* or on IRS Schedule C-EZ: *Net Profits of a Business* and are included in the calculations for completing the owner's joint or single IRS Form 1040.

The financial records that you will compile using the forms in this book will make your tax preparation much easier, whether you handle this yourself or it is handled by a tax professional. A basic comprehension of the information required on Federal tax forms will help you understand why certain financial records are necessary. Understanding tax reporting will also assist you as you decide how to organize your business financial records.

Please note that many of the tax forms mentioned in this section will only apply to sole proprietorships that actually hire employees. Simply because a sole proprietorship business is owned by one owner does not in any way restrict the sole owner from hiring employees or independent contractors to assist in the operation of the business. In fact, there have been sole proprietorships that have operated with many, many employees and at different locations and even in many states.

A checklist of tax forms is provided that details which IRS forms are necessary for this type of business. In addition, various schedules of tax filing are also provided to assist you in keeping your tax reporting timely.

C-Corporation Tax Forms Checklist

☐ IRS Form 1040, 1040-A, 1040-EZ: *U.S. Individual Income Tax Return.* One of these forms must be filed by all shareholders

☐ IRS Form 1120 or 1120-A: *U.S. Corporation Income Tax Return.* One of these forms must be filed by all C-corporations

☐ IRS Form 1120-W: *Estimated Tax for Corporations* (Worksheet). Must be completed by all corporations expecting a profit requiring estimated tax payments

☐ IRS Form SS-4: *Application for Employer Identification Number.* Must be filed by all C-corporations

☐ IRS Form W-2: *Wage and Tax Statement.* Must be filed by all C-corporations

☐ IRS Form W-3: *Transmittal of Wage and Tax Statement.* Must be filed by all C-corporations

☐ IRS Form W-4: *Employee's Withholding Allowance Certificate.* Must be provided to employees of C-corporations. It is not filed with the IRS

☐ IRS Form 940 or 940-EZ: *Employer's Annual Federal Unemployment Tax Return* (FUTA). Must be filed by all C-corporations

☐ IRS Form 941: *Employer's Quarterly Federal Tax Return.* Must be filed by all C-corporations

☐ IRS Form 8109: *Federal Tax Deposit Coupon.* Must be filed by all C-corporations with a monthly tax liability over $500.00

☐ Any required state and local income and sales tax forms. Please check with the appropriate tax authority for more information

C-Corporation Monthly Tax Schedule

☐ If corporate payroll tax liability is over $1000.00 monthly, the corporation must make monthly tax payments using IRS Form 8109

☐ If required, file and pay any necessary state or local sales tax

C-Corporation Quarterly Tax Schedule

☐ Pay any required corporate estimated taxes using IRS Form 8109

☐ File IRS Form 941 and make any required payments of FICA and withholding taxes

☐ If corporate unpaid FUTA tax liability is over $100.00, make FUTA deposit using IRS Form 8109

☐ If required, file and pay any necessary state or local sales tax

C Corporation Annual Tax Schedule

☐ Prepare W-2 Forms and provide to employees by January 31st and file Form W-3 and copies of all W-2 F)orms with IRS by January 31st

☐ If corporation has paid any independent contractors over $600.00 annually, prepare IRS Form 1099 and provide to recipients by January 31st and file IRS Form 1096 and copies of all 1099 forms with IRS by January 31st

☐ Make required unemployment tax payment and file IRS Form 940 (or 940-EZ)

☐ File IRS Form 1120 or 1120-A

☐ If required, file and pay any necessary state or local sales, income, or unemployment tax

Limited Liability Company Tax Forms Checklist
(Taxed as a Sole Proprietorship)

☐ IRS Form 1040: *U.S. Individual Income Tax Return*. Do not use IRS Form 1040-A or IRS Form 1040-EZ

☐ IRS Schedule C: *Profit or Loss from Business*. Must be filed with IRS Form 1040 by all limited liability companies electing to be treated as sole proprietorships, unless Schedule IRS Schedule C-EZ is filed

☐ IRS Schedule C-EZ: *Net Profit from Business*. May be filed if gross company receipts are under $25,000.00 and expenses are under $2,000.00

☐ IRS Form 1040-SS: *Self-Employment Tax*. Required for any sole proprietor who shows $400.00+ income from his or her limited liability company business on IRS Schedule C or C-EZ

☐ IRS Form 1040-ES: *Estimated Tax for Individuals*. Must be used by all companies that expect to make a profit requiring estimated taxes

☐ IRS Form SS-4: *Application for Employer Identification Number*. Must be filed by all companies who will hire one or more employees

☐ IRS Form W-2: *Wage and Tax Statement*. Must be filed by all companies that have one or more employees

☐ IRS Form W-3: *Transmittal of Wage and Tax Statement*. Must be filed by all companies that have one or more employees

☐ IRS Form W-4: *Employee's Withholding Allowance Certificate*. Must be provided to employees of companies. Not filed with the IRS

☐ IRS Form 940 or 940-EZ: *Employer's Annual Federal Unemployment Tax Return (FUTA)*. Must be filed by all companies that have employees

☐ IRS Form 941: *Employer's Quarterly Federal Tax Return.* Must be filed by all companies that have one or more employees

☐ IRS Form 8109: *Federal Tax Deposit Coupon.* Used by all companies with monthly employee tax liability over $500.00. (Obtain from IRS)

☐ IRS Form 8829: *Expenses for Business Use of Your Home.* Filed with annual IRS Form 1040, if necessary

☐ Any required state and local income and sales tax forms

Limited Liability Company Tax Forms Checklist (Taxed as a Partnership)

☐ IRS Form 1040: *U.S. Individual Income Tax Return.* Must be filed by all members. Do not use IRS Form 1040-A or IRS Form 1040-EZ

☐ IRS Form 1065: *U.S. Partnership Return of Income.* Must be completed by all limited liability companies which are taxed as partnerships

☐ IRS Schedule K-1: *Partner's Share of Income, Credit, Deductions, etc.* Must be filed by all members

☐ IRS Form 1040-SS: *Self-Employment Tax.* Required for any member who shows $400.00+ income from his or her business on Schedule K-1

☐ IRS Form 1040-ES: *Estimated Tax for Individuals.* Must be used by all members who expect to make a profit requiring estimated taxes

☐ IRS Form SS-4: *Application for Employer Identification Number.* Must be filed by all companies that will hire one or more employees

☐ IRS Form W-2: *Wage and Tax Statement.* Must be filed by all companies that have one or more employees

❏ IRS Form W-3: *Transmittal of Wage and Tax Statement.* Must be filed by all companies that have one or more employees

❏ IRS Form W-4: *Employee's Withholding Allowance Certificate.* Must be provided to employees of companies. Not filed with the IRS

❏ IRS Form 940 or 940-EZ: *Employer's Annual Federal Unemployment Tax Return (FUTA).* Must be filed by all companies that have employees

❏ IRS Form 941: *Employer's Quarterly Federal Tax Return.* Must be filed by all partnerships that have one or more employees

❏ IRS Form 8109: *Federal Tax Deposit Coupon.* Used by all companies with monthly employee tax liability over $500.00. (Obtain from IRS)

❏ Any required state and local income and sales tax forms. Please check with the appropriate tax authority for more information

Limited Liability Company Tax Forms Checklist (Taxed as a Corporation)

❏ IRS Form 8832: *Entity Classification Election.* This form must be completed and filed by all limited liability companies electing to be treated as a corporation

❏ IRS Form 1040: *U.S. Individual Income Tax Return.* Must be filed by all members. Do not use IRS Form 1040-A or IRS Form 1040-EZ

❏ IRS Form 1120 or 1120-A: *U.S. Corporation Income Tax Return.* One of these forms must be filed by all limited liability companies electing to be treated as a corporation

❏ IRS Form 1120-W: *Estimated Tax for Corporations* (Worksheet). Must be completed by all limited liability companies expecting a profit requiring estimated tax payments

☐ IRS Form SS-4: *Application for Employer Identification Number.* Must be filed by all limited liability companies

☐ IRS Form W-2: *Wage and Tax Statement.* Must be filed by all limited liability companies

☐ IRS Form W-3: *Transmittal of Wage and Tax Statement.* Must be filed by all limited liability companies

☐ IRS Form W-4: *Employee's Withholding Allowance Certificate.* Must be provided to employees of limited liability companies. It is not filed with the IRS

☐ IRS Form 940 or 940-EZ: *Employer's Annual Federal Unemployment Tax Return (FUTA).* Must be filed by all limited liability companies

☐ IRS Form 941: *Employer's Quarterly Federal Tax Return.* Must be filed by all limited liability companies

☐ IRS Form 8109: *Federal Tax Deposit Coupon.* Used by companies with monthly employee monthly tax liability over $500.00. (Obtain from IRS)

☐ Any required state and local income and sales tax forms. Please check with the appropriate tax authority for more information

Limited Liability Company
Monthly, Quarterly, and Annual Tax Schedules

Please use the appropriate tax schedules for the entity classification that you have chosen for your Limited Liability Company (i.e., Corporation, Partnership, or Sole Proprietorship). See the enclosed Forms-on-CD for the complete Limited Liability Company Tax Schedules.

Partnership Tax Forms Checklist

☐ IRS Form 1040: *U.S. Individual Income Tax Return.* Must be filed by all partners. Do not use IRS Form 1040-A or IRS Form 1040-EZ

☐ IRS Form 1065: *U.S. Partnership Return of Income.* Must be completed by all partnerships

☐ IRS Schedule K-1: *Partner's Share of Income, Credit, Deductions, etc.* Must be filed by all partners

☐ IRS Form 1040-SS: *Self-Employment Tax.* Required for any partner who shows $400.00+ income from the business on Schedule K-1

☐ IRS Form 1040-ES: *Estimated Tax for Individuals.* Must be used by all partners who expect to make a profit requiring estimated taxes

☐ IRS Form SS-4: *Application for Employer Identification Number.* Must be filed by all partnerships that will hire one or more employees

☐ IRS Form W-2: *Wage and Tax Statement.* Must be filed by all partnerships that have one or more employees

☐ IRS Form W-3: *Transmittal of Wage and Tax Statement.* Must be filed by all partnerships that have one or more employees

☐ IRS Form W-4: *Employee's Withholding Allowance Certificate.* Must be provided to employees of partnerships. It is not filed with the IRS

☐ IRS Form 940 or 940-EZ: *Employer's Annual Federal Unemployment Tax Return* (FUTA). Must be filed by all partnerships having employees

☐ IRS Form 941: *Employer's Quarterly Federal Tax Return.* Must be filed by all partnerships that have one or more employees

☐ IRS Form 8109: *Federal Tax Deposit Coupon.* Must be filed by all partnerships having employees and a monthly tax liability over $500.00

☐ Any required state and local income and sales tax forms. Please check with the appropriate tax authority for more information

Partnership Monthly Tax Schedule

☐ If you have employees, and your payroll tax liability is over $1,000.00 monthly, you must make monthly tax payments using IRS Form 8109

☐ If required, file and pay any necessary state or local sales tax

Partnership Quarterly Tax Schedule

☐ Pay any required estimated taxes using vouchers from IRS Form 1040-ES

☐ If you have employees: file IRS Form 941 and make any required payments of FICA and withholding taxes

☐ If you have employees and your unpaid FUTA tax liability is over $100.00, make a FUTA deposit using IRS Form 8109

☐ If required, file and pay any necessary state or local sales tax

Partnership Annual Tax Schedule

☐ If you have employees, prepare IRS Forms W-2 and provide to employees by January 31st and file Form W-3 and copies of all W-2 Forms with IRS by January 31st

☐ If you have paid any independent contractors over $600.00 annually, prepare IRS Form 1099 and provide to recipients by January 31st and file IRS Form 1096 and copies of all 1099 Forms with IRS by January 31st

❏ Make required unemployment tax payment and file IRS Form 940 (or 940-EZ)

❏ File IRS Form 1040-SS with your annual 1040 Form

❏ File IRS Form 1065 and IRS Schedule K-1

❏ If required, file and pay any necessary state or local sales, income, or unemployment tax

S-Corporation Tax Forms Checklist

❏ IRS Form 1040: *U.S. Individual Income Tax Return*. Must be filed by all S-corporation shareholders. Do not use IRS Form 1040-A or IRS Form 1040-EZ

❏ IRS Form 2553: *Election by a Small Business Corporation*. Must be filed by all S-corporations

❏ IRS Form 1120-S: *U.S. Income Tax Return for an S-Corporation*. Must be filed by all S-corporations

❏ IRS Schedule K-1: *Shareholder's Share of Income, Credit, Deductions, etc.* Must be completed by all S-corporations

❏ IRS Form 1040-ES: *Estimated Tax for Individuals*. Must be used by all S-corporation shareholders with a profit requiring estimated taxes

❏ IRS Form SS-4: *Application for Employer Identification Number*. Must be filed by all S-corporations

❏ IRS Form W-2: *Wage and Tax Statement*. Must be filed by all S-corporations

❏ IRS Form W-3: *Transmittal of Wage and Tax Statement*. Must be filed by all S-corporations

☐ IRS Form W-4: *Employee's Withholding Allowance Certificate*. Must be provided to employees of S-corporations. It is not filed with the IRS

☐ IRS Form 940 or 940-EZ: *Employer's Annual Federal Unemployment Tax Return* (FUTA). Must be filed by all S-corporations

☐ IRS Form 941: *Employer's Quarterly Federal Tax Return*. Must be filed by all S-corporations

☐ IRS Form 8109: *Federal Tax Deposit Coupon*. Must be filed by all S-corporations with a monthly tax liability over $500.00

☐ Any required state and local income and sales tax forms. Please check with the appropriate tax authority for more information

S-Corporation Monthly Tax Schedule

☐ If corporate payroll tax liability is over $1,000.00 monthly, the corporation must make monthly tax payments using IRS Form 8109

☐ If required, file and pay any necessary state or local sales tax

S-Corporation Quarterly Tax Schedule

☐ Pay any required estimated taxes using vouchers from IRS Form 1040-ES

☐ File IRS Form 941 and make any required payments of FICA and withholding taxes

☐ If corporate unpaid FUTA tax liability is over $100.00, make FUTA deposit using IRS Form 8109

☐ If required, file and pay any necessary state or local sales tax

S-Corporation Annual Tax Schedule

☐ Prepare W-2 Forms and provide to employees by January 31st and file Form W-3 and copies of all W-2 Forms with IRS by January 31st

☐ If corporation has paid any independent contractors over $600.00 annually, prepare IRS Forms 1099 and provide to recipients by January 31st and file IRS Form 1096 and copies of all 1099 Forms with IRS by January 31st

☐ Make required unemployment tax payment and file IRS Form 940 (or 940-EZ)

☐ File IRS Form 1120-S and IRS Schedule K-1

☐ If required, file and pay any necessary state or local sales, income, or unemployment tax

Sole Proprietorship Tax Forms Checklist

☐ IRS Form 1040: *U.S. Individual Income Tax Return*

☐ IRS Schedule C: *Profit or Loss from Business.* Must be filed with IRS Form 1040 by all sole proprietorships, unless IRS Schedule C-EZ is filed

☐ IRS Schedule C-EZ: *Net Profit from Business.* May be filed if gross receipts are under $25,000.00 and expenses are under $2,000.00

☐ IRS Form 1040-SS: *Self-Employment Tax.* Required for any sole proprietor who shows $400.00+ income from his or her business on IRS Schedule C or C-EZ

☐ IRS Form 1040-ES: *Estimated Tax for Individuals.* Must be used by all sole proprietors who expect to make a profit requiring estimated taxes

❏ IRS Form SS-4: *Application for Employer Identification Number.* Must be filed by all sole proprietors who will hire one or more employees

❏ IRS Form W-2: *Wage and Tax Statement.* Must be filed by all sole proprietors who have one or more employees

❏ IRS Form W-3: *Transmittal of Wage and Tax Statement.* Must be filed by all sole proprietors who have one or more employees

❏ IRS Form W-4: *Employee's Withholding Allowance Certificate.* Must be provided to employees of sole proprietors. Not filed with the IRS

❏ IRS Form 940 or 940-EZ: *Employer's Annual Federal Unemployment Tax Return* (FUTA). Must be filed by all sole proprietors who have employees

❏ IRS Form 941: *Employer's Quarterly Federal Tax Return.* Must be filed by all sole proprietors who have one or more employees

❏ IRS Form 8109: *Federal Tax Deposit Coupon.* Used by all employers with monthly employee tax liability over $500.00. (Obtain from IRS)

❏ IRS Form 8829: *Expenses for Business Use of Your Home.* Filed with annual IRS Form 1040, if necessary

❏ Any required state and local income and sales tax forms

Sole Proprietorship Monthly Tax Schedule

❏ If you have employees, and your payroll tax liability is over $1,000.00 monthly, you must make monthly tax payments using IRS Form 8109

❏ If required, file and pay any necessary state or local sales tax

Sole Proprietorship Quarterly Tax Schedule

☐ Pay any required estimated taxes using vouchers from IRS Form 1040-ES

☐ If you have employees, file IRS Form 941 and make any required payments of FICA and withholding taxes

☐ If you have employees and your unpaid FUTA tax liability is over $100.00, make FUTA deposit using IRS Form 8109

☐ If required, file and pay any necessary state or local sales tax

Sole Proprietorship Annual Tax Schedule

☐ If you have employees, prepare W-2 Forms and provide to employees by January 31st and file Form W-3 and copies of all W-2 Forms with IRS by January 31st

☐ If you have paid any independent contractors over $600.00 annually, prepare IRS Forms 1099 and provide to recipients by January 31st and file IRS Form 1096 and copies of all 1099 Forms with IRS by January 31st

☐ Make required unemployment tax payment and file IRS Form 940 (or 940-EZ)

☐ File IRS Form 1040-SS with your annual IRS Form 1040

☐ File IRS Schedule C or C-EZ with your annual IRS Form 1040

☐ File IRS Form 8829 with your annual IRS Form 1040, if necessary

☐ If required, file and pay any necessary state or local sales, income, or unemployment tax

Chapter 4

General Business Management Forms

The forms in this chapter are some basic general forms for use in the day-to-day operations of a small business. They may be used to keep track of phone calls and faxes as well as record phone messages and send with faxes. These forms can provide a business with important written records regarding the sending and receipt of phone calls and faxes. Such records may be vitally important should questions ever arise regarding details about messages sent or received by the company. Following are brief descriptions:

Fax Cover Sheet: This is a basic sheet that can be sent with each fax that details the recipient and sender of the fax, as well as the topic and length of the fax.

Telephone Call Record: This form provides a method to track each phone call made, including date, caller, recipient, and phone number.

Fax Record: Similar to the above form, but intended to track faxed messages.

Mail Sent Log: The details regarding the sending of important letters or packages may be tracked with the information added to this form.

Mail Receipt Log: The receipt of important mail may be tracked by filling out this form for each package or letter received.

Memo: Provides a written record of messages to employees or management.

Phone Memo: Similarly, this form provides for a written record of phone call messages to company employees or staff.

Fax Cover Sheet

Date: _____

From:
Company:

To:
Company:

Number of pages transmitted (including this page):
If transmission incomplete or error, please call:

Message:

_____
Signature

_____
Name

Telephone Call Record

Date	Caller	Call to	Company/Address	City	Phone Number	Charges

Notes:

Fax Record

Date	Faxed by	Fax to	Company/Address	City	Phone Number	Charges

Notes:

Mail Sent Log

Date	Sender	Company/Address	City/State/Zip	Contents	Charges	

Notes:

Mail Receipt Log

Date	Recipient	Sender	Company/Address	City/State/Zip	Contents

Notes:

Memo

Date:
To:
From:
Subject:

☐ Urgent
☐ Please Respond
☐ For your info
☐
☐
☐

When finished, please route to:
_____
_____
_____

Phone Memo

Call for:
Call from:
Company:

Date:
Time:
Phone: (   )

☐ AM   ☐ PM

Message:

Action:

☐ Phoned
☐ Please call back
☐ Returned your call
☐ Will call again

Message taken by:

Chapter 5

Marketing Forms

An integral part of the process of starting a business is preparing a marketing plan. Whether the business will provide a service or sell a product, it will need customers in some form. Who those customers are, how they will be identified and located, and how they will be attracted to the business are crucial to the success of any small business. Unfortunately, it is also one part of a business start-up that is given less than its due in terms of time and effort spent to fully investigate the possibilities. In this chapter, four marketing forms are provided to assist you in thinking about your business in terms of who the customers may be and how to reach them. In many ways, looking honestly at who your customers may be and how to attract them may be the most crucial part of your business. For if your understanding of this issue is ill-defined or unclear, your business will have a difficult time succeeding.

The following four forms are provided to help in defining your business marketing strategy:

- Competitive Analysis Form
- Marketing Strategy Form
- Sales and Pricing Analysis Form
- Target Marketing Analysis Form

By completing these forms, you should be able to create a clear and straightforward description of your own businesses marketing objectives and methods.

Competitive Analysis Form

Who are your main competitors?_____

Are there competitors in the same geographic area as your proposed business? _____

Are the competitors successful and what is their market share? _____
_____

How long have they been in business?_____

Describe your research into your competitors' business operations: _____
_____

Are there any foreseeable new competitors? _____
_____

What are the strengths and/or weaknesses of your competitor's product/service? _____

Why is your product/service different or better than that of your competitors (or worse!)?_____

What is the main way that you will compete with your competitors (price, quality, technology, advertising, etc.)?_____
_____

How will your customers know that your product/service is available? ___
_____

What is the main message that you want your potential customers to receive? _____

Why is your product/service unique? _____
_____

How will you be able to expand your customer base over time?_____
_____

Marketing Strategy Form

What is your annual projected marketing budget? _____
_____

Have your company's logo, letterhead, and business cards already been de-signed? _____
_____

Do you have a company slogan or descriptive phrase? _____

Has packaging for your product/service been designed?_____

Has signage for your facility been designed?_____

Describe your advertising plans:
Signs:	_____
Brochures:	_____
Catalogs:	_____
Yellow Pages:	_____
Magazines:	_____
Trade journals:	_____
Radio:	_____
Television:	_____
Newspapers:	_____
Internet:	_____
Trade shows:	_____
Videos:	_____
Billboards:	_____
Newsletters:	_____

Have advertisements already been designed? _____

Have you prepared a media kit for publicity? _____

Describe your plans to receive free publicity in the media via news releases or new product/service releases:
Radio:	_____
Television:	_____

Newspapers: _____

Magazines: _____

Internet: _____

Have you requested inclusion in any directories, catalogs, or other marketing vehicles for your industry?_____

Describe any planned direct mail campaigns:_____

_____

Describe any planned telemarketing campaigns:_____

_____

Describe any Internet-based marketing plans:

E-mail account: _____

_____

Web site: _____

_____

Will there be any special or seasonal promotions of your product/service?

_____

How will your customers actually receive the product/service?_____

_____

Sales and Pricing Analysis Form

What are your competitors' prices for similar products/services? _____

Are your prices higher or lower, and why? _____

Will you offer any discounts for quantity or other factors? _____

Will you accept checks and/or credit cards for payment? _____

Will you have a sales force? Describe: _____

What skills or education will the sales force need? _____

Will there be sales quotas? _____

Will the sales force be paid by salary, wages, or commission? _____

Are there any geographic areas or limitations on your sales or distribution?
_____

Will you sell through distributors or wholesalers? Describe: _____

Will there be dealer margins or wholesale discounts? _____

Do you have any plans to monitor customer feedback? Describe: _____
_____

Do you have warranty, guarantee, and customer return policies? Describe:
_____

Will any customer service be provided? Describe: _____

What is your expected sales volume for the first five years?
Year one: _____
Year two: _____
Year three: _____
Year four: _____
Year five: _____

Target Marketing Analysis Form

What is the target market for your product/service? _____

_____

What types of market research have you conducted to understand your market?

_____

_____

What is the geographic market area you will serve? _____

_____

Describe a typical customer:
    Sex: _____
    Marital status: _____
    Age: _____
    Income: _____
    Geographic location: _____
    Education: _____
    Employment: _____

Estimate the number of potential people in the market in your area of service:

_____

What is the growth potential for this market? _____

_____

How will you satisfy the customers' needs with your product/service? _____

_____

Will your product/service make your customers' life more comfortable? _____

_____

Will your product/service save your customers' time or money or stress? _____

_____

Chapter 6

Business Credit Documents

The forms which are contained in this chapter relate to the extension of business credit to customers. In many business situations it is customary to offer credit to continuing customers on mutually-agreeable terms. The prudent businessperson, however, should take certain steps to assure that the company that is being offered credit is a sound business risk. The various forms provided allow for the collection of credit information and for the evaluation of the credit potential of business customers.

Business Credit Application: This form is the basis of a check into the credit history of a customer. With this form a company desiring credit furnishes various information which may be checked further to ascertain the reliability and background of the credit applicant.

The credit applicant is requested to furnish the following information:

- Company name and address and length of time in business
- Gross annual sales, net profits, and net value of the company
- Type of business
- Three bank references
- Three trade references
- Three credit references

In addition, the applicant is asked to request a credit limit for their account. Finally, the various credit terms which are being applied for are spelled out. The following information will need to be filled in before sending the form to a potential credit customer: the interest rate on overdue balances, and number of days within which an invoice is to be paid.

Notice of Approval of Business Credit Application: This form is used to approve the above credit application. It should be sent only after the information in the credit application has been thoroughly checked and approved. This form reiterates the credit terms that your company is offering to the applicant.

Request for Bank Credit Reference: This form is intended to be used to contact the various banking references that a credit applicant has offered in her or his Business Credit Application. It requests the bank to provide confidential information regarding the applicant's banking and credit history with the bank. A copy of the applicant's Business Credit Application should be attached to this request when sending it to the bank.

Request for Trade Credit Reference: This form is intended to be used to contact the various trade references that a credit applicant has offered in her or his Business Credit Application. It requests that the trade vendor provide confidential information regarding the applicant's banking and credit history with the vendor. A copy of the applicant's Business Credit Application should be attached to this request when sending it to the vendor.

Request for Credit Information: This final form is designed to be used to obtain information regarding your personal credit history from any credit reporting agency. It is in accordance with the Federal Fair Credit Reporting Act. Fill in the appropriate information and forward it to the credit reporting agency from which you wish to obtain information.

Business Credit Application

Company Name _____

Billing Address _____

Phone _____ Fax _____ Telex _____

e-mail Address _____

____ Corporation   ____ Partnership   ____ Proprietorship   ____ Other

Type of Business _____ Year Established _____

Yearly Gross Sales $ _____ Yearly Net Profits $ _____ Net Value $ _____

NAMES AND ADDRESSES OF OWNERS, PARTNERS, OR OFFICERS:

Name _____ SS # _____ Title _____

Address _____

Name _____ SS # _____ Title _____

Address _____

Name _____ SS # _____ Title _____

Address _____

CREDIT REFERENCES:

Creditor Name _____ Account # _____ Phone_____

Address _____

Creditor Name _____ Account # _____ Phone_____

Address _____

Creditor Name _____ Account # _____ Phone_____

Address _____

TRADE CREDIT REFERENCES:

Vendor Name _____ Account # _____ Phone_____

Address _____

Vendor Name _____ Account # _____ Phone_____

Address _____

Vendor Name _____ Account # _____ Phone_____
Address _____

BANK REFERENCES:

Bank Name _____ Account # _____ Phone_____
Address _____

Bank Name _____ Account # _____ Phone_____
Address _____

Bank Name _____ Account # _____ Phone_____
Address _____

CREDIT LIMIT REQUESTED: $ _____

CREDIT TERMS:
- Payment on all invoices is due within ____ days of invoice date.
- All overdue invoices bear interest at ____ % (_____ percent) per month on unpaid balance.
- Credit applicant agrees to pay all costs of collection, including court costs and attorneys fees.
- Credit terms and limit may be cancelled or changed by Creditor at any time without notice.
- All transactions are governed by the laws of the Creditor's state.
- All transactions are governed by the terms of the Creditor's documents.

The Credit applicant accepts the above terms and states that all information contained in this credit application is true and correct. Credit applicant authorizes creditor to contact all references, inquire as to credit information, and receive any confidential information relevant to approving credit.

Dated: _____ , 20 ____

_____
Signature of Credit Applicant

_____
Name of Credit Applicant

Notice of Approval of Business Credit Application

Date: _____

To:

RE: Credit Application

Dear _____ :

Please be advised that, based upon your credit application which you filed with our firm dated _____ , 20 ____ , your credit has been approved.

Please be further advised that your initial credit limit is $ _____ .

The terms of this extension of credit to your company are as follows:
- Payment on all invoices is due within ____ days of invoice date.
- All overdue invoices bear interest at ____ % (_____ percent) per month on unpaid balance.
- Credit applicant agrees to pay all costs of collection, including court costs and attorneys fees.
- Credit terms and limit may be cancelled or changed by Creditor at any time without notice.
- All transactions are governed by the laws of the Creditor's state.
- All transactions are governed by the terms of the Creditor's documents.

If you have any questions regarding this matter, please contact our accounting department. Thank you very much and we look forward to doing business with you.

Very truly,

_____
Signature

_____
Name

Request for Bank Credit Reference

Date: _____

To:

RE: Credit Reference for _____ ,
     Account Number _____ .

The above-named company has filed a credit application with our company naming your bank as a credit reference. By that application, the credit applicant has authorized us to contact the stated references and receive confidential information from them regarding their credit history. Attached please find a copy of the Credit Application naming your bank as a reference and authorizing our company to receive credit information.

We would, therefore, appreciate it if you could provide us with the following information:

1. How long has the company had an account with your bank?
2. What has been the average daily account balance?
3. Is there a history of overdrafts on this account?
4. Does this company currently have any loans with your bank?

   (a) If so, what is the outstanding balance?
   (b) Are they secured loans?
   (c) What is the collateral?
   (d) Has the repayment been satisfactory?

5. Has this customer been a satisfactory banking client?

We would appreciate any further information that you might be able to provide that may enable us to evaluate the credit history of this applicant. All information will be held in strict confidence. Thank you very much for your assistance.

_____
Signature

_____
Name

Request for Trade Credit Reference

Date: _____

To:

RE: Credit Reference for _____ ,
     Account Number _____ .

The above-named company has filed a credit application with our company naming your company as a credit reference. By that application, the credit applicant has authorized us to contact the stated references and receive confidential information from them regarding their credit history. Attached please find a copy of the Credit Application naming your company as a reference and authorizing our company to receive credit information.

We would, therefore, appreciate it if you could provide us with the following information:

1. How long has the company had an account with your company?
2. What has been the average credit line of this company?
3. Is there a history of past due payments by this company?
4. What is the current credit balance owed you by this company?
5. Has the repayment been satisfactory?
6. What are the credit terms that you have extended to this customer?
7. Has this customer been a satisfactory customer?

We would appreciate any further information that you might be able to provide that may enable us to evaluate the credit history of this applicant. All information will be held in strict confidence. Thank you very much for your assistance.

_____
Signature

_____
Name

Request for Credit Information

To:

RE: Disclosure of Credit Information

By this letter, I hereby request complete disclosure of my personal credit file as held within your agency records. This request is in accordance with the Federal Fair Credit Reporting Act. I request that this disclosure provide the names and addresses of any parties who have received a copy of my credit report, and the names and addresses of any parties who have provided information that is contained in my credit report.

Name _____

Prior or other name _____

Address _____

Prior or other address _____

Social Security Number _____ Phone _____

Dated: _____ , 20 ____

_____
Signature

_____
Name

State of _____
County of _____

On _____ , 20 ___ , _____ personally came before me and, being duly sworn, did state that she/he is the person described in the above document and that she/he signed the above document in my presence.

_____
Notary Public, In and for the County of _____
State of _____
My commission expires: _____

193

Chapter 7

Business Financing Documents

The documents included in this chapter are designed for use in situations in which businesspersons will be using personal property as collateral for a loan. Loans for real estate, other than a simple promissory note and mortgage or trust deed, are generally subject to more state regulations and, thus, should be handled by a real estate professional or attorney.

The legal documents for financing of business loans generally employ three key documents, each of which serves a different purpose. First, there is the actual *promissory note (secured)* by which the borrower promises to repay a debt. Next is the *security agreement* by which the borrower puts up specific property as collateral for repayment of a loan. Finally, there is the *U.C.C. financing statement* that is used to record a lien against personal property in the public records.

All states have adopted a version of the Uniform Commercial Code (U.C.C.). This code is a set of detailed regulations which govern the purchase and sale of goods and financing arrangements, along with many other commercial transactions. Every state has a method of filing (on the public record) various statements relating to financing arrangements. The value of making timely filings of financing statements and other U.C.C. related matter is that the date and time of filing the statement *perfects* (or legally locks in time) the security interest that has been bargained for. The party with the earliest perfected security interest relating to a particular piece of property has priority claim to that property. The various forms included in this chapter are as follows:

Promissory Note (Secured): This type of promissory note is referred to as a *secured* note. What this means is that the borrower has given the noteholder some form of property or right to property as collateral for the loan. This allows the noteholder a direct claim against the specific property and the ability to foreclose against the property if the note is in default. A secured note also places the noteholder higher on the list for repayment if the borrower files for bankruptcy.

This particular form is designed to be used in conjunction with a completed Security Agreement covering the security arrangement between the borrower and the noteholder (lender). The security for this type of note must be personal property. A secured promissory note may be drawn up for use with real estate as collateral. However, since this will entail the use of a mortgage or deed of trust as the security agreement, the services of a lawyer or real estate professional may be required. This secured promissory note is set up for installment payments, if desired. The conditions of this promissory note are as follows:

- That default on any of the conditions of the underlying security agreement may allow the noteholder to demand immediate full payment on the note
- That the borrower may prepay any amount on the note without penalty
- That if the borrower is in default, the noteholder may demand full payment on the note
- That the note is not assumable by anyone other than the borrower
- That the borrower waives certain formalities relating to demands for payment
- That the borrower agrees to pay any of the costs of collection after a default

The following information is needed to complete this form:

- The names and addresses of the borrower and the noteholder
- The amount of the principal of the loan
- The annual interest rate to be charged
- The period for the installments (for example, monthly or weekly)
- The day of the period on which payments will be due
- The date of the security agreement which coincides with the note
- The number of days a payment may be late before it is considered a default

Security Agreement: This document is the document that provides the *secured party* (the party providing a loan) with the right to the collateral that the borrower has put up as security for the repayment of the loan. The security agreement in this book provides for the following terms:

- That the borrower is granting the secured party a security interest in the property named
- That the security interest is to secure payment of a certain obligation
- That if the borrower defaults on the obligation, the secured party may accelerate the loan and make it immediately due and payable

195

- That if the borrower defaults, the secured party will have all the remedies under the U.C.C. (these may include selling the property or keeping the property)
- That the borrower will pay any costs of collection upon default
- That the borrower will be careful with the collateral and will not sell or dispose of it
- That the borrower will insure the collateral and keep it at a specified address for the term of the loan period
- That the borrower states that the property is owned free and clear, with no other liens against it, and that they have authority to use it as collateral
- That the borrower will sign any necessary financing statements
- That any changes to the agreement must be in writing

Receipt for Collateral: If it is desired that the property offered as collateral be held by the secured party, it will be necessary to alter the above Security Agreement by deleting Paragraphs 5 and 6 and preparing this receipt for the collateral. This receipt provides:

- That the secured party has obtained the collateral and will hold it as security until the loan is repaid
- That if the borrower defaults on the obligation, the property may be disposed of to satisfy the obligation
- That the borrower will pay any costs and expenses relating to holding the property
- That the secured party does not acknowledge the value or condition of the property offered as collateral

General Guaranty: This form provides for a guarantor for the repayment of a debt. This *guarantor* is, in effect, a co-signer for the obligation. The guarantor agrees that if any of the payments are late or not paid, they will make the payments. The guarantor also agrees to pay any costs of collection if the guaranty is not lived up to. The guarantor also agrees that the guaranty may be enforced without having to first sue the borrower for defaulting on the debt. A mere default by the borrower without any court action will suffice to require the guarantor to make good on the obligation. To fill in this form, use the names and addresses of the borrower, noteholder, and guarantor, and the number of days payment by the guarantor may be late before it is considered a default on the guaranty.

Financing Statement (U.C.C.): This form is a memorandum of the details of a security arrangement. It is designed to be filed with the appropriate state filing office in order to record the security interest. Once filed, this statement serves as a public record of the date and time that the security interest in the particular property was perfected. To fill in this form, simply provide the names and addresses of the parties and a description of the security interest being filed.

Release of Security Interest: This form acts as a release of property from its nature as collateral for a loan. In addition, when the loan is repaid, the note or obligation should also be released. To fill in this form, simply provide the names and addresses of the parties and a description of the security interest being released.

Release of U.C.C. Financing Statement: This form is a memorandum detailing the release of a financing obligation and should be filed with the state filing office to clear the records once the obligation has been satisfied. To fill in this form, provide the names and addresses of the parties and a description of the financing statement being released.

Release of Promissory Note: This release is intended to be used to release a party from obligations under a Promissory Note. There are several other methods by which to accomplish this same objective. The return of the original note to the maker, clearly marked "Paid In Full" will serve the same purpose. A Receipt for Full Payment will also accomplish this goal. The Release of Promissory Note may, however, be used in those situations when the release is based on something other than payment in full of the underlying note. For example, the note may be satisfied by a gift from the bearer of the note of release from the obligation. Another situation may involve a release of the note based on a concurrent release of a claim which the maker of the note holds against the holder of the note.

Promissory Note (Secured)

$ _____

Dated: _____ , 20 ____

For value received, the Borrower, _____ , of _____ ,
City of _____ , State of _____ , promises to pay to the Noteholder, _____ , of _____ , City of _____ ,
State of _____ , the principal amount of $ _____ , with interest at
the annual rate of ____ % (_____ percent) on any unpaid balance.

Payments are payable to the Noteholder in _____ consecutive installments of $ _____ , including interest, and continuing on the _____
day of each _____ until paid in full. If not paid off sooner, this
Note is due and payable in full on _____ , 20 ____ .

This Note is secured by a Security Agreement dated _____ ,
20 ____ , which has also been signed by the Borrower. This Note may be
accelerated and demand for immediate full payment made by the Noteholder upon breach of any conditions of the Security Agreement. This
Note may be prepaid in whole or in part at any time without penalty. If
the Borrower is in default more than _____ days with any payment, this
Note is payable upon demand of any Noteholder. This note is not assumable without the written consent of the Noteholder. The Borrower waives
demand, presentment for payment, protest, and notice. In the event of any
default, Borrower will be responsible for any costs of collection on this
Note, including court costs and attorney fees.

_____
Signature of Borrower

_____
Name of Borrower

Security Agreement

This Agreement is made on _____ , 20 ____ , between _____ , Borrower, of _____ , City of _____ , State of _____ , and _____ , Secured Party, of _____ , City of _____ , State of _____ .

For valuable consideration, the parties agree as follows:

1. The Borrower grants the Secured Party a security interest under Article 9 of the Uniform Commercial Code in the following personal property which will be considered Collateral:

2. This security interest is granted to secure payment by the Borrower to the Secured Party on the following obligation:

3. In the event of default by the Borrower in payment of any of the amounts due on the obligation listed under Paragraph 2, the Secured Party may declare the entire obligation immediately due and payable and will have all of the remedies of a secured party under the Uniform Commercial Code.

4. In the event of such default, Borrower will also be responsible for any costs of collection, including court costs and attorney fees.

5. The Borrower agrees to use reasonable care in using the Collateral and agrees not to sell or dispose of the Collateral.

6. The Borrower agrees to keep the Collateral adequately insured and at the following address for the entire term of this Security Agreement:

7. The Borrower represents that the Collateral is owned free and clear and that there are no other security agreements, indebtedness, or liens relating to the property offered as Collateral. Borrower also states that it has full authority to grant this security interest.

8. Borrower agrees to sign any financing statements that are required by the Secured Party to perfect this security interest.

9. No modification of this Agreement will be effective unless it is in writing and is signed by both parties. This Agreement binds and benefits both parties and any successors.

10. Time is of the essence of this agreement. This document, including any attachments, is the entire agreement between the parties. This Agreement is governed by the laws of the State of _____ .

The parties have signed this Agreement on the date specified at the beginning of this Agreement.

_____
Signature of Borrower

_____
Name of Borrower

_____
Signature of Secured Party

_____
Name of Secured Party

Receipt for Collateral

This receipt is made in connection with the Promissory Note dated
_____ , 20 ____ , and the Security Agreement dated
_____ , 20 ____ , between the Borrower, _____ , of
_____ , City of _____ , State of _____ ,
and the Noteholder/ Secured Party, _____ , of _____ ,
City of _____ , State of _____ .

The Noteholder/Secured Party acknowledges delivery of the following described personal property as collateral under the Security Agreement:

This collateral is subject to the lien and all of the conditions of the Security Agreement. In the event of the Borrower's default on any of the terms of the Note or Security Agreement, this property may be disposed of by the Noteholder/Secured Party to satisfy any of the Borrower's obligations as allowed by law.

The Borrower will continue to pay all costs and expenses relating to this property, including any maintenance, storage fees, insurance, or taxes.

This receipt does not acknowledge the condition or the value of the property retained as collateral.

Dated: _____ , 20 ____

_____
Signature of Borrower

_____
Name of Borrower

_____
Signature of Secured Party/Noteholder

_____
Name of Secured Party/Noteholder

General Guaranty

This Guaranty is made in connection with the Promissory Note dated
_____ , 20 ____ , and the Security Agreement dated
_____ , 20 ____ , between the Guarantor, _____ , of
_____ , City of _____ , State of _____ ,
and the Noteholder/Secured Party, _____ , of _____ ,
City of _____ , State of _____ .

For value received, the Guarantor unconditionally guarantees payment of all payments on the above Promissory Note when due and satisfaction of all terms of the Security Agreement.

The Guarantor waives demand, presentment for payment, protest, and notice, and agrees that the Secured Party/Noteholder does not have to exhaust all rights against the Borrower before demanding payment under this guaranty.

In the event that all payments due under this Guaranty are not paid on demand within _____ days of demand, Guarantor will also be responsible for any costs of collection on this Note, including court costs and attorney fees.

This Guaranty both binds and benefits both parties and any successors.

Dated: _____ , 20 ____

_____
Signature of Guarantor

_____
Name of Guarantor

_____
Signature of Secured Party/Noteholder

_____
Name of Secured Party/Noteholder

Financing Statement (U.C.C.)

This Original Financing Statement is presented for filing under the Uniform Commercial Code as adopted in the following state: _____ .

(This Section for Use of the Filing Officer)

Date of filing _____   Time of filing _____

Number and address of filing office _____
_____
_____

Name(s) of Borrower _____
Address(es) of Borrower _____
Name(s) of Secured Party _____
Address(es) of Secured Party _____

This Financing Statement covers the following personal property:

This Financing Statement secures a debt document described as:

Name of document _____   Date of document _____
Face value of document $ _____   Maturity date _____

Related terms and conditions of the debt are contained in this debt document and any other documents mentioned in the debt document.

Dated: _____ , 20 ____

_____
Signature of Borrower

                                        SEAL

_____
Name of Borrower

Release of Security Interest

For valuable consideration, _____ , of _____ , City of _____ , State of _____ , releases _____ , of _____ , City of _____ , State of _____ , from the following specific Security Agreement, dated _____ , 20 ____ :

Any claims or obligations that not specifically mentioned are not released by this Release of Security Interest.

The Secured Party has not assigned any claims or obligations covered by this release to any other party.

The Secured Party will sign a Release of U.C.C. Financing Statement if requested by Borrower.

The party signing this release intends that it both bind and benefit any successors.

Dated: _____ , 20 ____

_____
Signature of Secured Party

_____
Name of Secured Party

Release of U.C.C. Financing Statement

This Release of Financing Statement is presented for filing under the Uniform Commercial Code as adopted in the following state: _____ .

(This Section for Use of the Filing Officer)

Date of filing _____   Time of filing _____

Number and address of filing office _____
_____
_____

Name(s) of Borrower _____
Address(es) of Borrower _____
Name(s) of Secured Party _____
Address(es) of Secured Party _____

The Original Financing Statement covers the following personal property:

File Number of Original Financing Statement _____

Dated: _____

Office where Original Financing Statement was filed _____

Dated: _____ , 20 ____

_____
Signature of Secured Party

                                        SEAL

_____
Name of Secured Party

State of _____
County of _____

On _____ , 20 ____ , _____ personally came before me and, being duly sworn, did state that he/she is the person described in the above document and that he/she signed the above document in my presence.

_____
Notary Public, In and for the County of _____
State of _____
My commission expires: _____

Release of Promissory Note

In consideration of full payment of the promissory note dated _____ , 20 ____ in the face amount of $ _____ , the Noteholder, _____ , of _____ , City of _____ , State of _____ , releases and discharges the Borrower(s), _____ , of _____ , City of _____ , State of _____ , from any claims or obligations on account of this note.

The party signing this release intends that it bind and benefit both itself and any successors.

Dated: _____ , 20 ____

_____
Signature of Noteholder

_____
Name of Noteholder

Chapter 8

Collection Documents

The documents contained in this chapter are for use in the collection of past-due payments owed to you. Through the proper use of the documents in this chapter, your business should be able to collect on the majority of overdue and unpaid accounts without having to resort to the use of attorneys or collection agencies. Of course, if the initial attempts at collection using these documents fail, then it is advisable to turn the accounts over to parties who will be able to bring legal procedures to bear on the defaulting parties. The following forms are included in this chapter:

Request for Payment: This form should be used to make the initial request for payment from an overdue account payable. It should be sent when you have decided that an account is in delinquent status. It is intended to promote payment on the overdue account. To prepare this form, you will need to enter the name of the company or person with the delinquent account; the date, amount, and invoice numbers of the past-due invoices; any interest or late charges which have been assessed; and any credits or payments which have been made on the account. Be sure to keep a record of this request. Generally, making a copy of the actual request that is sent and placing in the file for the overdue account is the easiest method for this.

Second Request for Payment: You will generally use this form on the next billing date after you have sent the first request for payment. The information necessary for this form will be the same as the first request. You will need, however, to update any additions or subtractions to the account which have taken place during the period since the first request (for example, any payments on account, additional interest charges, additional late payments, additional invoices, etc.).

Final Demand for Payment: This form should normally be used after one more billing cycle has elapsed since the second payment request was sent. It is a notice that collection proceedings will be begun if payment has not been received on the delinquent account within 10 days. (Please note that you may extend this period if you desire, for example, to allow for 30 days to pay). This notice should not be sent unless you actually plan on following up with the collection. However, it is often reasonable to wait a short while after the deadline before proceeding with assignment of the account for collection. This allows for delays in mail delivery and takes into account the tendency of companies and people with debt problems to push the time limits to the maximum.

Assignment of Account for Collection: This document is one of the methods to follow-up the final demand for payment. With this document, the past-due account is entirely turned over to either a collection agency or attorney for further collection procedures. This form is an actual assignment of the account to the firm who then actually owns the account and will continue any attempts at collection. It provides that the *Assignee* (the firm who will be taking over the collection procedures) pays your company (the *Assignor*, or the "one who assigns") an amount for the rights to collect the account. The fee paid is generally a percentage of the amount due. For example, if the fee is fifty percent and you are owed $4,000.00 on the account, the Assignee firm will pay you $2,000.00 for taking over the account. Of course, if they are successful in collecting the entire amount they will have earned an additional $2,000.00. But at least you will have gotten half of the money owed to you. Under this method of collection, all future payments are to be paid to the Assignee firm. Another method for handling collection is provided below in the "Appointment of Collection Agent" form.

Notice of Assignment of Account for Collection: This form is used to notify the customer that the past-due account has been formally assigned to the collection firm. It tells the customer to make future payments on the account to the collection firm.

Appointment of Collection Agent: Through the use of this document, you appoint a collection agency to collect the delinquent account. This method of collection differs slightly from the actual assignment of the account for collection, in that the appointment of the agent for collection is only for a limited period of time and the fee which the collection agent earns is entirely dependent upon their ability to actually collect the money which is owed to you. This is known as a *contingent* fee arrangement. The collection agent may act on your behalf in attempting to collect the account, but does not have actual ownership of the account. You may limit the actions that the agent takes or spell out specific steps you wish taken with the special instructions. Generally, the payments will continue to be made to your company.

Notice of Appointment of Collection Agent: This form should be used in conjunction with the above form. While the appointment form above is used between your business and the collection service, this form should be used to notify the delinquent account of the appointment of the collection agent for their account. It instructs the customer to make payments to your company or contact the collection agent.

Notice of Disputed Account: This form should be used by you if you have received a statement with which you disagree. If you feel that the statement is in error, spell out your reasoning in the space provided and send this form to the creditor.

Offer to Settle Disputed Account: This form is also intended to be used by your company if you dispute a statement sent to you by others. Through the use of this form, you can offer a compromise settlement on the account. A check in the amount of your compromised settlement can safely be sent with this offer, since, by the terms of the offer, cashing the check will be acceptance of the offer to compromise. Many companies will jump at the cash in hand and agree to concede the remaining balance. This document should only be used if there is an actual dispute regarding the amount owed.

Agreement to Settle Disputed Account: This is a formal version of the above letter agreement. This form may be used to spell out the terms of the compromise settlement more clearly. It should be used by your company if you have received an informal settlement offer from another party to settle an account.

Notice of Dishonored Check: This document should be sent to anyone whose bad check has been returned to you from a bank. It is generally a good idea to attempt to have the check cleared twice before beginning the collection process with this letter. This provides time for last minute deposits to clear and will often allow the check to clear. This document gives notice to the person of the dishonored check, notifies them of your policy and charges regarding service charges for bad checks, and provides a time limit for clearing up the bad check prior to legal action. Once the check has been paid, return the original check to the debtor.

Notice of Default on Installment Promissory Note: This form will be used to notify the maker of a promissory note of their default on an installment payment on a promissory note. Notice of default should be sent promptly to any account which falls behind in their payments on a note. It provides a legal basis for a suit for breach of the promissory note.

Demand for Full Payment on Installment Promissory Note: A demand for full payment on a promissory note can only be made if the precise terms of the note allow for this. A note may have specific terms which allow it to be accelerated upon default on any payments. This means that if the maker of the note falls behind on their payments, the holder may *accelerate* all of the payment dates to the present and demand that the note be paid in full. Generally, this form will be used after giving the debtor a reasonable time to make up the missed installment payment.

Demand for Payment on Demand Promissory Note: This document should be used when you hold a promissory note which is payable on demand and you wish to demand full payment. Realistically, you should generally allow the maker of such a note a reasonable amount of time to gather enough funds to make the payment. This form allows a period of 10 days. However, you may wish to modify this period after consulting with the debtor.

Demand for Payment on Promissory Note Guarantor: This form is intended for use if the defaulted-upon note has been guaranteed by a third party. Any such guaranty should, generally, be clearly noted on the face of the note. This demand notifies the guarantor of the default of the *maker* of the note (the borrower) and demands that the guarantor live up to the promise to pay upon the default of the maker.

Stop Payment on Check Order: This form is intended to be provided to a bank or similar financial institution to confirm a telephone stop payment request. This form provides the institution with written confirmation of the oral request to stop payment on a check.

Request for Payment

Date: _____

To:

RE: Payment of Account

Dear _____ :

Regarding your account, please be advised that we show the following outstanding balance on our books:

Invoice # _____   Date _____   Amount $ _____
Invoice # _____   Date _____   Amount $ _____
Interest on account at ____ % (_____ percent)   Amount $ _____
Late charges   Amount $ _____
Less credits and payments   Amount $ _____

TOTAL BALANCE DUE   AMOUNT $ _____

Please be advised that we have not yet received payment on this outstanding balance. We are certain that this is merely an oversight and would ask that you please send the payment now. Please disregard this notice if full payment has been forwarded to us.

Thank you for your immediate attention to this matter.

Very truly,

_____
Signature

_____
Name

Second Request for Payment

Date: _____

To:

RE: Payment of Account

Dear _____ :

Regarding your account, please be advised that we continue to show the following outstanding balance on our books:

Invoice # _____   Date _____   Amount $ _____
Invoice # _____   Date _____   Amount $ _____
Interest on account at ____ % (_____ percent)   Amount $ _____
Late charges   Amount $ _____
Less credits and payments   Amount $ _____

TOTAL BALANCE DUE   AMOUNT $ _____

Please be advised that since our last request for payment dated _____ , 20 ____ , we have still not yet received payment on this outstanding balance. We must request that you please send the payment immediately. Please disregard this notice if full payment has been forwarded to us.

Thank you for your immediate attention to this matter.

Very truly,

_____
Signature

_____
Name

Final Demand for Payment

Date: _____

To:

RE: Payment of Account

Dear _____ :

Regarding your delinquent account in the amount of $ _____ , we have requested payment on this account several times without success.

THIS IS YOUR FINAL NOTICE.

Please be advised that unless we receive payment in full on this account in this office within 10 (ten) days of the date of this letter, we will immediately turn this account over to our attorneys for collection proceedings against you without further notice.

These proceedings will include claims for pre-judgment interest on your account and all legal and court-related costs in connection with collection of this past-due account and will substantially increase the amount which you owe us. Collection proceedings may also have an adverse effect on your credit rating.

We regret the necessity for this action and urge you to clear up this account delinquency immediately. If full payment has been sent, please disregard this notice.

Thank you for your immediate attention to this serious matter.

Very truly,

_____
Signature

_____
Name

Assignment of Account for Collection

This Assignment is made on _____ , 20 ____ , by and between _____ , Assignor, of _____ , City of _____ , State of _____ , and _____ , Assignee, of _____ , City of _____ , State of _____ . It is regarding the Account Receivable due to the Assignor from a customer of Assignor, known as _____ , Customer, of _____ , City of _____ , State of _____ . As of this Date, the Account Receivable balance is $ _____ .

For valuable consideration, the parties agree as follows:

1. The Assignee agrees to pay to the Assignor on this day the sum of $ _____ , in return for which the Assignor assigns all right, title, and interest in this Account Receivable to the Assignee for collection.

2. Assignor shall indemnify and hold harmless the Assignee from any and all claims arising from the Account receivable or the underlying contract between the Assignor and the Customer. Assignor agrees to furnish the Assignee all information required by the Assignee in its collection efforts. Assignor agrees to notify the Customer of this Assignment and to pay to the Assignee any payments on this account which are received from Customer after this date.

Dated _____ , 20 ____

_____

Signature of Assignor

_____

Name of Assignor

_____

Signature of Assignee

_____

Name of Assignee

Notice of Assignment of Account for Collection

Date: _____

To:

RE: Assignment of Account for Collection

Dear _____ :

Please be advised that as of _____ , 20 ____ , the following account receivable balance has been assigned for collection to the firm of _____ , of _____ , City of _____ , State of _____ .

Invoice # _____   Date _____   Amount $ _____
Invoice # _____   Date _____   Amount $ _____
Interest on account at ____ % (_____ percent)   Amount $ _____
Late charges   Amount $ _____
Less credits and payments   Amount $ _____

TOTAL BALANCE DUE   AMOUNT $ _____

Please contact the above firm regarding all future payments on this account.

Very truly,

_____
Signature

_____
Name

Appointment of Collection Agent

This Agreement is made on _____ , 20 ____ , by and between _____ , Seller, of _____ , City of _____ , State of _____ , and _____ , Agent, of _____ , City of _____ , State of _____ . It is regarding the Account Receivable due to the Seller from a customer of Seller, known as _____ , Customer, of _____ , City of _____ , State of _____ . As of this date, the Account Receivable balance is $ _____ .

For valuable consideration, the parties agree as follows:

1. Seller appoints Agent to collect this Account Receivable from Customer on behalf of Seller. Agent will be entitled to a contingent fee of ____ % (_____ percent) of whatever amount of the Account Receivable is collected by the Agent, payable to the Agent upon receipt of the collected amounts. Agent is also subject to the following special instructions:

2. Seller shall indemnify and hold harmless the Agent from any and all claims arising from the Account Receivable or the underlying contract between the Seller and the Customer. Agent shall indemnify and hold harmless the Seller from any and all claims arising from the Agent's collection efforts. Seller agrees to furnish the Agent all information required by the Agent in its collection efforts. Seller agrees to notify the Customer of this Appointment.

Dated _____ , 20 ____

_____
Signature of Seller

_____
Name of Seller

_____
Signature of Agent

_____
Name of Agent

Notice of Appointment of Collection Agent

Date: _____

To:

RE: Appointment of Collection Agent

Dear _____ :

Please be advised that as of _____ , 20 ____ , the firm of
_____ , located at _____ , City of _____ ,
State of _____ , has been appointed as agent for collection of
the following account receivable balance:

Invoice # _____   Date _____   Amount $ _____
Invoice # _____   Date _____   Amount $ _____
Interest on account at ____ % (_____ percent)   Amount $ _____
Late charges   Amount $ _____
Less credits and payments   Amount $ _____

TOTAL BALANCE DUE   AMOUNT $ _____

You may continue to make your payments to our company or you may
make further payment to the collection agent. Thank you.

Very truly,

_____
Signature

_____
Name

Notice of Disputed Account

Date: _____

To:

RE: Account Payable

Dear _____ :

We are in receipt of your statement of our account dated _____ ,
20 ____ , indicating a balance due you of $ _____ .

We dispute this amount due for the following reasons:

Please contact us immediately to discuss the adjustment of our account.

Very truly,

_____
Signature

_____
Name

Offer to Settle Disputed Account

Date: _____

To:

RE: Account Payable

Dear _____ :

We are in receipt of your statement of our account dated _____ ,
20 ____ , indicating a balance due you of $ _____ .

As noted in our previous letter dated _____ , 20 ____ , we dispute this amount due for the following reasons:

Without admitting any liability on this account, but as an offer to compromise the amount due, we offer to settle this account in full by our
payment to you of $ _____ .

Our check number _____ in that amount is enclosed. Your deposit of that
check shall confirm your acceptance of our offer to settle this account
and shall discharge the entire balance claimed.

Very truly,

_____

Signature

_____

Name

Agreement to Settle Disputed Account

This Agreement is made on _____ , 20 ____ , by and between
_____ , Seller, of _____ , City of _____ ,
State of _____ , and _____ , Customer, of
_____ , City of _____ , State of _____, regard-
ing a disputed Account Payable dated _____ , 20 ____ , in the
amount of $ _____ , based on the following invoices:

For valuable consideration, the parties agree as follows:

1. The Seller will accept a lesser payment of $ _____ , in full settlement
    of the claim on this account.

2. If the Customer does not pay the Seller this lesser payment within 10
    (ten) days of receipt of a signed original copy of this Agreement, the
    Seller may sue the Customer for the full amount of the disputed Ac-
    count Payable.

3. If the Customer pays the lesser payment within the time allowed for
    payment, both parties mutually release each other from any and all
    claims or rights to sue each other arising from their dispute over pay-
    ment of this Account Payable.

4. This Agreement binds and benefits both parties and any successors.

Dated _____ , 20 ____

_____
Signature of Seller

_____
Name of Seller

_____
Signature of Customer

_____
Name of Customer

Notice of Dishonored Check

Date: _____

To:

RE: Dishonored Check

Dear _____ :

Please be advised that payment on your Check number _____ , dated
_____ , 20 ____ , in the amount of $ _____ , has been refused by
your bank, _____ , of _____ , City of _____ ,
State of _____ . We have verified with your bank that there are
insufficient funds to pay the check.

Therefore, we request that you immediately replace this check with cash
or a certified check for the amount of the bad check and an additional
$ _____ as our service charge.

Unless we receive such payment within 10 (ten) days from the date of this
letter, or such further time as may be allowed by state law, we will immediately commence appropriate legal action for recovery of our funds.
Please be advised that such legal proceedings may substantially increase
the amount owed to us and may include pre-judgment interest and legal
and court costs.

Upon receipt of payment, we will return your check to you. Thank you for
your prompt response to this serious matter.

Very truly,

_____
Signature

_____
Name

Notice of Default on Installment Promissory Note

Date: _____

To:

RE: Default on Promissory Note Payment

Dear _____ :

Regarding the Promissory Note dated _____ , 20 _____ , in the original amount of $ _____ , of which you are the maker, you have defaulted on the installment payment due on _____ , 20 _____ , in the amount of $ _____ .

Demand is made upon you for payment of this past-due installment payment. If payment is not received by us within 10 (ten) days from the date of this notice, we will proceed to enforce our rights under the Promissory Note for collection of the entire balance.

Very truly,

_____
Signature

_____
Name

Demand for Full Payment on Installment Promissory Note

Date: _____

To:

RE: Demand for Payment on Note

Dear _____ :

I am currently the holder of your Promissory Note dated _____ ,
20 ____ , in the amount of $ _____ , which is payable to _____ .

You have been given previous notice on _____ , 20 ____ , of
your default on payments of this Note. Under the terms of the Note and by
this notice, I am making a formal demand for payment by you of the full
unpaid balance of this Note, together with all accrued interest within 10
(ten) days of receipt of this letter.

Please contact me at the following address and phone number in order
to initiate the payment process:

If full payment is not received within 10 (ten) days from the date of this
Demand, the Note shall be forwarded to our attorneys for legal collection
proceedings and you will be immediately liable for all costs of collection,
including additional legal and court costs. Thank you very much for your
prompt attention to this serious matter.

Very truly,

_____

Signature

_____

Name

Demand for Payment on Demand Promissory Note

Date: _____

To:

RE: Demand for Payment on Note

Dear _____ :

I am currently the holder of your Promissory Note dated _____ ,
20 _____ , in the amount of $ _____ , which is payable to _____ ,
or to the holder on demand.

By this notice, I am making a formal demand for payment by you of the
full unpaid balance of this Note, together with all accrued interest, within
10 (ten) days of receipt of this letter. The total amount due at this time is
$ _____ .

Please contact me at the following address and phone number in order
to initiate the payment process:

If full payment is not received within 10 (ten) days from the date of this
Demand, the Note shall be forwarded to our attorneys for legal collection
proceedings and you will be immediately liable for all costs of collection,
including any additional legal and court costs. Thank you very much for
your prompt attention to this serious matter.

Very truly,

_____
Signature

_____
Name

Demand for Payment on Promissory Note Guarantor

Date: _____

To:

RE: Demand for Payment on Note

Dear _____ :

I am currently the holder of a Promissory Note dated _____ , 20 ____ , in the amount of $ _____ , of which the Maker is _____ , and of which you are the Guarantor. This Note is payable to _____ , or to the holder on demand.

Please be advised that on _____ , 20 ____ , notice and demand for payment was made to the Maker and payment has not been forthcoming. By this notice, I am making a formal demand for immediate payment by you of the full unpaid balance of this Note, together with all interest.

Please contact me at the following address and phone number in order to initiate the payment process:

If full payment is not received within 10 (ten) days from the date of this Demand, the Note shall be forwarded to our attorneys for legal collection proceedings and you will be immediately liable for all costs of collection, including any additional legal and court costs. Thank you very much for your prompt attention to this serious matter.

Very truly,

_____
Signature

_____
Name

Stop Payment on Check Order

Date: _____

To:

RE: Stop Payment on Check

Dear _____ :

Pursuant to our telephone conversation of _____ , 20 ____ ,
please stop payment on the following check:

Account name	_____
Account number	_____
Check number	_____
Check date	_____
Check amount	_____
Payable to	_____

Thank you for your immediate attention to this matter.

Very truly,

_____

Signature

_____

Name

Chapter 9

Purchase of Goods Documents

The documents in this chapter are all related to the purchase and sale of goods from the perspective of the business doing the purchasing. The purchase and sale of goods in business situations is governed by the Uniform Commercial Code as it has been adopted by the various states. The forms in this chapter are intended to be used to comply with the provisions of the U.C.C. and protect your rights.

Request for Price Quote: This form is used to obtain a firm price quote for particular goods. It allows the purchaser to lock in the price for a certain time period and bars the seller from raising the price during that period.

Notice of Acceptance of Order: This form provides for acceptance of an order and acknowledgment that the order has been inspected and approved by the purchaser.

Notice of Conditional Acceptance of Nonconforming Goods: When a purchaser receives a shipment of goods that does not conform to the order that was placed, the purchaser may offer to accept the goods on the condition that the purchase price be adjusted to accommodate for the nonconformity of the goods. The seller, of course, has the right to reject any discount and request that the goods be returned. This form allows for a conditional acceptance of the goods and requests that a price reduction be allowed within 10 days.

Notice of Rejection of Nonconforming Goods: Use this form after the above form has been used and the 10-day period for acceptance of the price reduction terms has expired. This forms notifies the seller that the goods have been fully rejected for nonconformity with the original purchase order. It also gives the seller 10 days to return the money paid for the goods and 10 days to arrange for return of the goods. If the money is not returned, the advice of an attorney versed in business law should be sought.

Notice of Conditional Acceptance of Defective Goods: When a purchaser receives a shipment of goods that is defective or damaged in some manner, the purchaser may offer to accept the goods on the condition that the purchase price be adjusted to accommodate for the defect in the goods. The seller, of course, has the right to reject any discount and request that the goods be returned. This form allows for a conditional acceptance of the goods and requests that a price reduction be allowed within 10 days.

Notice of Rejection Of Defective Goods: This form should be used after using the above form and after the 10-day period for acceptance of the price reduction terms has expired. This form notifies the seller that the goods have been fully rejected for defects. It also gives the seller 10 days to return the money paid for the goods and 10 days to arrange for return of the goods. If the money is not returned, the advice of an attorney versed in business law should be sought.

Notice of Rejection of Order: This form is a generic form for the rejection of an order by the purchaser. In addition to rejection of an order for non-conformity or for defective goods, orders may be rejected for unreasonable delay in shipment, damage, partial shipment only, that the price charged was not what was quoted, etc. It gives the seller 10 days to return the money paid for the goods. If the money is not returned, the advice of a business attorney should be sought.

Notice of Refusal to Accept Delivery: This form should be used in those situations when the actual delivery of the goods is rejected (for example, when physical damage is evident on immediate inspection).

Notice of Demand for Delivery of Goods: The use of this form is required in situations in which goods have been ordered and paid for, but not delivered. This notifies the seller of a demand for immediate shipment of the goods or return of the money.

Notice of Cancellation of Purchase Order: After the use of the above form notifying the seller of a demand for delivery of goods and after the expiration of the 10 day period set for delivery by the above notice, this form should be sent to the seller. It effectively cancels the original purchase order for non-delivery and demands the return of any money paid. If the money is not returned, the advice of an attorney competent in business law should be sought.

Notice of Return of Goods Sold on Approval: When a purchaser receives goods "on approval," they are allowed to examine the goods for a certain period and return them to the seller if desired within that time frame. This form is used to notify the seller of the decision to return the goods sold on approval.

Request for Price Quote

Date: _____

To:

RE: Request for Price Quote

Dear _____ :

We are interested in purchasing the following goods:

Please provide us with a firm quote for your standard price for these goods and the time period during which this quote will be good. Also, please provide us with your discount schedule for volume purchases. Please also provide us with the following information regarding any order that we might place with your company:

1. The standard terms for payment of invoices
2. The availability of an open credit account with your firm. (If available, please provide us with the appropriate credit application)
3. Any delivery costs for orders. (If these costs are included in the price quote, please indicate)
4. Any sales or other taxes. (If these costs are included in the price quote, please indicate)
5. The usual delivery time for orders from the date of your receipt of a purchase order to our receipt of the goods

Very truly,

_____

Signature

_____

Name

Notice of Acceptance of Order

Date: _____

To:

RE: Acceptance of Order

Dear _____ :

Please be advised that we have received the following goods, pursuant to our purchase order number _____ , dated _____ , 20 _____ :

The goods are further identified by invoice number _____ and bill of lading/packing slip number _____ .

Please be advised that we have inspected the goods and they have been received in good condition, with no defects, and in conformity with our order.

Accordingly, we accept this shipment of goods.

Thank you.

Very truly,

_____
Signature

_____
Name

Notice of Conditional Acceptance of Nonconforming Goods

Date: _____

To:

RE: Conditional Acceptance of Nonconforming Goods

Dear _____ :

On _____ , 20 ____ , we received delivery from you on our purchase order number _____ , dated _____ , 20 ____ . The goods which were delivered at that time do not conform to the specifications that were provided with our purchase order for the following reasons:

Although these goods are nonconforming and we are not obligated to accept them, we are prepared to accept these goods on the condition that you credit our account with you for $ _____ . This credit will make the total price of the goods under this purchase order $ _____ .

If you do not accept this proposal within 10 (ten) days from the date of this notice, we will reject these goods as nonconforming and they will be returned to you.

Please be advised that we reserve all of our rights under the Uniform Commercial Code and any other applicable laws.

Thank you for your immediate attention to this matter.

Very truly,

_____
Signature

_____
Name

Notice of Rejection of Nonconforming Goods

Date: _____

To:

RE: Rejection of Nonconforming Goods

Dear _____ :

On _____ , 20 ____ , we received delivery from you on our purchase order number _____ , dated _____ , 20 ____ . The goods which were delivered at that time do not conform to the specifications that were provided with our purchase order for the following reasons:

We paid for these goods by our check number _____ , dated _____ , 20 ____ , in the amount of $ _____ . This check has been cashed by you.

By this notice, we reject the delivery of these goods and demand the return of our money. Unless we receive a refund of our money within 10 (ten) days of the date of this letter, we will take immediate legal action for the return of our money.

Please further advise us as to your wishes for the return of the rejected goods at your expense. Unless we receive return instructions within 10 (ten) days of this letter, we accept no responsibility for their safe storage.

Please be advised that we reserve all of our rights under the Uniform Commercial Code and any other applicable laws.

Thank you for your immediate attention to this matter.

Very truly,

_____

Signature

_____

Name

Notice of Conditional Acceptance of Defective Goods

Date: _____

To:

RE: Conditional Acceptance of Defective Goods

Dear _____ :

On _____ , 20 ____ , we received delivery from you on our purchase order number _____ , dated _____ , 20 ____ . The goods which were delivered at that time were defective for the following reasons:

Although these goods are defective and we are not obligated to accept them, we are prepared to accept these goods on the condition that you credit our account with you for $ _____ . This credit will make the total price of the goods under this purchase order $ _____ .

If you do not accept this proposal within 10 (ten) days from the date of this notice, we will reject these goods as defective and they will be returned to you.

Please be advised that we reserve all of our rights under the Uniform Commercial Code and any other applicable laws.

Thank you for your immediate attention to this matter.

Very truly,

_____
Signature

_____
Name

Notice of Rejection of Defective Goods

Date: _____

To:

RE: Rejection of Defective Goods

Dear _____ :

On _____ , 20 _____ , we received delivery from you on our purchase order number _____ , dated _____ , 20 _____ . The goods which were delivered at that time were defective for the following reasons:

We paid for these goods by our check number _____ , dated _____ , 20 _____ , in the amount of $ _____ . This check has been cashed by you.

By this notice, we reject the delivery of these goods and demand the return of our money. Unless we receive a refund of our money within 10 (ten) days of the date of this letter, we will take immediate legal action for the return of our money.

Please further advise us as to your wishes for the return of the rejected goods at your expense. Unless we receive instructions for their return within 10 (ten) days of this letter, we accept no responsibility for their safe storage.

Please be advised that we reserve all of our rights under the Uniform Commercial Code and any other applicable laws.

Thank you for your immediate attention to this matter.

Very truly,

_____
Signature

_____
Name

Notice of Rejection of Order

Date: _____

To:

RE: Rejection of Order

Dear _____ :

On _____ , 20 ____ , we received delivery from you on our purchase order number _____ , dated _____ , 20 ____ . We reject these goods for the following reasons:

We paid for these goods by our check number _____, dated _____ , 20 ____ , in the amount of $ _____. This check has been cashed by you.

By this notice, we reject the delivery of these goods and demand the return of our money. Unless we receive a refund of our money within 10 (ten) days of the date of this letter, we will take immediate legal action for the return of our money.

Please further advise us as to your wishes for the return of the rejected goods at your expense. Unless we receive instructions for their return within 10 (ten) days of this letter, we accept no responsibility for their safe storage.

Please be advised that we reserve all of our rights under the Uniform Commercial Code and any other applicable laws.

Thank you for your immediate attention to this matter.

Very truly,

_____
Signature

_____
Name

Notice of Refusal to Accept Delivery

Date: _____

To:

RE: Refusal to Accept Delivery

Dear _____ :

On _____ , 20 ____ , we received delivery from you on our purchase order number _____ , dated _____ , 20 ____ . We do not accept delivery of these goods for the following reasons:

We paid for these goods by our check number _____ , dated _____ , 20 ____ , in the amount of $ _____ . This check has been cashed by you.

By this notice, we refuse to accept the delivery of these goods and demand the return of our money. Unless we receive a refund of our money within 10 (ten) days of the date of this letter, we will take immediate legal action for the return of our money.

Please be advised that we reserve all of our rights under the Uniform Commercial Code and any other applicable laws.

Thank you for your immediate attention to this matter.

Very truly,

_____
Signature

_____
Name

Notice of Demand for Delivery of Goods

Date: _____

To:

RE: Demand for Delivery of Goods

Dear _____ :

On _____ , 20 _____ , by our purchase order number _____ , a copy of which is enclosed, we ordered the following goods from you:

We paid for these goods by our check number _____ , dated _____ , 20 _____ , in the amount of $ _____ . This check has been cashed by you.

To date, the goods have not been delivered to us. We, therefore, demand the immediate delivery of these goods. Unless the goods are delivered to us within 10 (ten) days of the date of this letter, we will take action to cancel this purchase order and have our money returned.

Please be advised that we reserve all of our rights under the Uniform Commercial Code and any other applicable laws.

Thank you for your immediate attention to this matter.

Very truly,

_____
Signature

_____
Name

Notice of Cancellation of Purchase Order

Date: _____

To:

RE: Cancellation of Purchase Order

Dear _____ :

On _____ , 20 ____ , by our purchase order number _____ , a copy of which is enclosed, we ordered the following goods from you:

We paid for these goods by our check number _____ , dated _____ , 20 ____ , in the amount of $ _____ . This check has been cashed by you.

On _____ , 20 ____ , we demanded immediate delivery of the goods. To date, the goods have not been delivered to us.

By this notice, we, therefore, cancel this order for late delivery and demand the immediate return of our money. Unless we receive a refund of our money within 10 (ten) days of the date of this letter, we will take immediate legal action for the return of our money.

Please be advised that we reserve all of our rights under the Uniform Commercial Code and any other applicable laws.

Thank you for your immediate attention to this matter.

Very truly,

_____
Signature

_____
Name

Notice of Return of Goods Sold on Approval

Date: _____

To:

RE: Return of Goods Sold on Approval

Dear _____ :

On _____ , 20 ____ , by our purchase order number
_____ , a copy of which is enclosed, we received the following
goods from you on approval:

Please be advised that at this time we are electing to return these goods
to you.

Thank you very much for the opportunity to examine the goods.

Very truly,

_____
Signature

_____
Name

Chapter 10

Sale of Goods Documents

The various forms included in this chapter are also intended to be used for situations involving the sale of goods. However, these forms are prepared for use by the seller. The first set are forms to be used in response to a buyer's action after goods have been shipped. Two legal contracts relating to the sale of goods are also included

Demand for Explanation of Rejected Goods: Use of this form will follow a seller's notification that the buyer has rejected goods. It demands a satisfactory explanation for the rejection. To complete this form, specify the date, purchase order number, and type of goods shipped, and date of rejection of the goods.

Notice of Replacement of Rejected Goods: This notice is to be used to replace goods that have been reasonably rejected by a buyer. It also instructs the buyer to return the rejected goods at the seller's expense. To complete this form, specify the date, purchase order number, and type of goods shipped, and date of rejection of the goods.

Notice of Goods Sold on Approval: When goods are sold to a buyer on approval, this form should be used to specify the time period that the buyer has to examine the goods and either accept or return them.

Contract for Sale of Goods: This basic contract is for the one-time sale of specific goods. To properly complete this document, the following information is necessary:

- The names and addresses of the seller and buyer
- A description of the goods being sold
- Any specifications that the buyer wishes to place on the goods
- The cost of the goods and the terms of payment
- The delivery date required by the buyer

- The amount of shipping costs and which party is to pay for the shipping
- Any additional terms of the sale
- The state whose laws will govern the contract

Contract for Sale of Goods on Consignment: For the sale of goods to a buyer on *consignment* (for resale), this form should be used. It provides that the seller will deliver goods to the buyer and that the buyer will display and attempt to resell the goods. It also provides that the goods remain the property of the seller until sold and that the buyer must return any unsold goods on demand. The following information will be used to prepare this document:

- The names and addresses of the seller and buyer
- A description of the goods being sold
- The cost of the goods and the terms of payment
- The price set for the goods
- The amount of shipping costs and which party is to pay for the shipping
- Any additional terms of the sale
- The state whose laws will govern the contract

Demand for Explanation of Rejected Goods

Date: _____

To:

RE: Demand for Explanation of Rejected Goods

Dear _____ :

On _____ , 20 _____ , we shipped the following goods to you pursuant to your purchase order number _____ , dated _____ , 20 _____ :

On _____ , 20 _____ , we received notice that you had rejected delivery of these goods without satisfactory explanation. We, therefore, request that you provide us with an adequate explanation for this rejection. Unless we are provided with such explanation within 10 (ten) days, we will take legal action to obtain payment for these goods.

Please be advised that we reserve all of our rights under the Uniform Commercial Code and any other applicable laws.

Thank you for your immediate attention to this matter.

Very truly,

_____
Signature

_____
Name

Notice of Replacement of Rejected Goods

Date: _____

To:

RE: Notice of Replacement of Rejected Goods

Dear _____ :

On _____ , 20 ____ , we shipped the following goods to you pursuant to your purchase order number _____ , dated _____ , 20 ____ :

On _____ , 20 ____ , we received notice that you had rejected delivery of these goods.

Please return the rejected goods to us at our expense using the same carrier that delivered the goods.

In addition, please be advised that we are shipping replacement goods to you at our expense.

If this correction of the rejected goods is not satisfactory, please contact us immediately. We apologize for any problems this may have caused.

Very truly,

_____
Signature

_____
Name

Notice of Goods Sold on Approval

Date: _____

To:

RE: Goods Sold on Approval

Dear _____ :

Please be advised that the following goods are being delivered to you on approval:

If these goods do not meet your requirements, you may return all or a part of them at our expense within _____ days of your receipt of the goods.

Any of these goods sold on approval that have not been returned to us by that time will be considered accepted by you and you will be charged accordingly.

We trust that you will find our goods satisfactory. Thank you very much for your business.

Very truly,

_____
Signature

_____
Name

Contract for Sale of Goods

This Contract is made on _____ , 20 ____ , between
_____ , Seller, of _____ , City of _____ ,
State of _____ , and _____ , Buyer, of _____ ,
City of _____ , State of _____ .

For valuable consideration, the parties agree as follows:

1. The Seller agrees to sell and the Buyer agrees to buy the following
   goods:

2. The Seller agrees to provide goods which meet the following specifications:

3. The Buyer agrees to pay the following price for the goods:

4. The Seller agrees that the goods will be delivered to the Buyer's place
   of business by _____ , 20 ____ . The shipping costs are
   estimated at $ _____ , and will be paid by the _____ .

5. The Seller represents that it has legal title to the goods and full authority to sell the goods. Seller also represents that the property is sold free
   and clear of all liens, mortgages, indebtedness, or liabilities.

6. Any additional terms:

7. No modification of this Contract will be effective unless it is in writing and is signed by both parties. Time is of the essence of this Contract. This Contract binds and benefits both the Buyer and Seller and any successors. This document, including any attachments, is the entire agreement between the Buyer and Seller. This Contract is governed by the laws of the State of _____ .

The parties have signed this Contract on the date specified at the beginning of this Contract.

_____
Signature of Seller

_____
Name of Seller

_____
Signature of Buyer

_____
Name of Buyer

Contract for Sale of Goods on Consignment

This Contract is made on _____ , 20 ____ , between
_____ , Seller, of _____ , City of _____ ,
State of _____ , and _____ , Buyer, of _____ ,
City of _____ , State of _____ .

For valuable consideration, the parties agree as follows:

1. The Seller agrees to provide the following goods to the Buyer on consignment:

2. The Buyer agrees to display the goods at its place of business and use its best efforts to re-sell the goods at the following price:

3. The goods will remain the property of the Seller until they are re-sold by the Buyer. The Buyer agrees to pay the following price to the Seller for any goods sold while held on consignment under this Contract:

4. The Seller agrees that the goods will be delivered to the Buyer's place of business by _____ , 20 ____ . The shipping costs are estimated at $ _____ , and will be paid by the _____ (Buyer or Seller).

5. The Buyer agrees to return any unsold goods, in good condition, to the Seller on the Seller's written demand.

6. The Seller represents that it has legal title to the goods and full authority to sell the goods. Seller also represents that the property is sold free and clear of all liens, mortgages, indebtedness, or liabilities.

7. Any additional terms:

8. No modification of this Contract will be effective unless it is in writing and is signed by both parties. Time is of the essence of this contract. This Contract binds and benefits both the Buyer and Seller and any successors. This document, including any attachments, is the entire agreement between the Buyer and Seller. This Contract is governed by the laws of the State of _____ .

The parties have signed this Contract on the date specified at the beginning of this Contract.

_____
Signature of Seller

_____
Name of Seller

_____
Signature of Buyer

_____
Name of Buyer

Chapter 11

Receipts

In this chapter, various receipt forms are provided. Receipts are a formal acknowledgment of having received something, whether it is money or property. The following forms are included in this chapter:

Receipt in Full: This form should be used as a receipt for a payment which completely pays off a debt. You will need to include the amount paid, the name of the person who paid it, the date when paid, and a description of the obligation which is paid off (for example: an invoice, statement, sales slip, note, or bill of sale). The original receipt should go to the person making the payment, but a copy should be retained.

Receipt on Account: This form should be used as a receipt for a payment which does not fully pay off a debt, but, rather, is a payment on account and is credited to the total balance due. You will need to include the amount paid, the name of the person who paid it, the date when paid, and a description of the account to which the payment is to be applied. The original receipt should go to the person making the payment, but a copy should be retained.

Receipt for Goods: This form should be used as a receipt for the acceptance of goods. It is intended to be used in conjunction with a delivery order or purchase order. It also states that the goods have been inspected and found to be in conformance with the order. The original of this receipt should be retained by the person delivering the goods and a copy should go to the person accepting delivery.

Receipt in Full

The undersigned acknowledges receipt of the sum of $ _____ paid by _____ . This payment constitutes full payment and satisfaction of the following obligation:

Dated: _____ , 20 ____

_____
Signature of Person Receiving Payment

_____
Name of Person Receiving Payment

Receipt on Account

The undersigned acknowledges receipt of the sum of $ _____ paid by _____ . This payment will be applied and credited to the following account:

Dated: _____ , 20 ____

_____
Signature of Person Receiving Payment

_____
Name of Person Receiving Payment

Receipt for Goods

The undersigned acknowledges receipt of the goods which are described on the attached purchase order. The undersigned also acknowledges that these goods have been inspected and found to be in conformance with the purchase order specifications.

Dated: _____ , 20 ____

_____
Signature of Person Receiving Goods

_____
Name of Person Receiving Goods

Index

★ Nova Publishing Company ★
Small Business and Consumer Legal Books and Software

Small Business Library Series

Simplified Small Business Accounting (2nd Edition)
ISBN 0-935755-61-6   Book only $19.95
The Complete Book of Small Business Legal Forms (3rd Edition)
ISBN 0-935755-84-5   Book w/Forms-on-CD $24.95
Incorporate Your Business: The National Corporation Kit (3rd Edition)
ISBN 0-935755-88-8   Book w/Forms-on-CD $24.95
The Complete Book of Small Business Management Forms
ISBN 0-935755-56-X   Book w/Forms-on-CD $24.95

Small Business Start-up Series

C-Corporations: Small Business Start-up Kit
ISBN 0-935755-78-0   Book w/Forms-on-CD $24.95
S-Corporations: Small Business Start-up Kit
ISBN 0-935755-77-2   Book w/Forms-on-CD $24.95
Partnerships: Small Business Start-up Kit
ISBN 0-935755-75-6   Book w/Forms-on-CD $24.95
Limited Liability Company: Small Business Start-up Kit
ISBN 0-935755-76-4   Book w/Forms-on-CD $24.95
Sole Proprietorship: Small Business Start-up Kit
ISBN 0-935755-79-9   Book w/Forms-on-CD $24.95

Quick Reference Law Series

Bankruptcy Exemptions: Laws of the United States
ISBN 0-935755-71-3   Book only $16.95
Corporations: Laws of the United States
ISBN 0-935755-67-5   Book only $16.95
Divorce: Laws of the United States
ISBN 0-935755-68-3   Book only $16.95
Limited Liability Companies: Laws of the United States
ISBN 0-935755-80-2   Book only $16.95
Partnerships: Laws of the United States
ISBN 0-935755-69-1   Book only $16.95
Wills and Trusts: Laws of the United State
ISBN 0-935755-70-5   Book only $16.95

Legal Self-Help Series

Debt Free: The National Bankruptcy Kit (2nd Edition)
ISBN 0-935755-62-4   Book only $19.95
The Complete Book of Personal Legal Forms (3rd Edition)
ISBN 0-935755-92-6   Book w/Forms-on-CD $24.95
Divorce Yourself: The National No-Fault Divorce Kit (4th Edition)
ISBN 0-935755-63-2   Book only $24.95
ISBN 0-935755-64-0   Book w/Forms-on-Disk $34.95
Prepare Your Own Will: The National Will Kit (5th Edition)
ISBN 0-935755-72-1   Book only $17.95
ISBN 0-935755-73-X   Book w/Forms-on-CD $27.95

★ Ordering Information ★

Distributed by:
National Book Network
4720 Boston Way
Lanham MD 20706

Shipping/handling: $4.50 for first book or disk and $.75 for each additional
Phone orders with Visa/MC: (800) 462-6420
Fax orders with Visa/MC: (800) 338-4550
Internet: www.novapublishing.com (in association with Amazon.com)